how to
Teach
Pronunciation

Gerald Kelly

Longman

series editor:
Jeremy Harmer

Pearson Education Limited
Edinburgh Gate
Harlow
Essex CM20 2JE
England
and Associated Companies throughout the world.

www.longman.com

First published 2000
Seventh impression 2004

Printed in Malaysia, PP

Produced for the publishers by Bluestone Press, Charlbury, Oxfordshire, UK. Text design by Keith Rigley. Copy-edited by Sue Harmes. Illustrations on page 26 by Maggie Hollings. All other illustrations by Bob Farley (Graham-Cameron Illustration).

ISBN 0582 429757

Contents

For Frank and Moira Kelly, who would've been chuffed.

Acknowledgements

Thanks to all the colleagues, trainees and students I have worked with over the years, who have influenced the ideas contained in this book in ways they may or may not be aware of. Thanks also to those who have trained me, for sparking off and then containing my enthusiasm for pronunciation teaching. Spare a thought for those friends and colleagues who have listened to me talk about precious little else over a long period of time.

Thanks are also due to the following:

Hester and David Lott for their excellent editing and guidance in shaping the final text.

All those at Longman who have been involved in the production of this book.

Andy Hopkins, for his insightful comments on the German language.

Coffee producers worldwide!

Last, but certainly not least, enormous thanks to K for keeping me fed, watered and sane, and to Emily, Alice and Rosie for keeping the sun shining.

Introduction

Who is this book for?

How to Teach Pronunciation has been written for all teachers of English who wish to improve their knowledge and develop their practical skills in this important area.

What is this book about?

This book aims to help teachers gain theoretical knowledge and to confirm and extend what they already know. It also suggests a variety of practical ideas, skills and activities for the classroom. The book shows teachers how to integrate pronunciation work with the treatment of grammar and lexis in order to help students appreciate its relevance and importance for successful communication.

- Chapter 1 explores the features and physiology of pronunciation, and introduces phonemic transcription.
- Chapter 2 deals with various approaches to teaching pronunciation, and introduces three types of lesson: Integrated lessons, where pronunciation is fully integrated with the other aspects of the language being taught; Remedial lessons and activities, which deal with pronunciation difficulties and issues which arise in class; and Practice lessons and activities, where particular aspects of pronunciation are addressed in their own right.
- Chapters 3 to 8 separate out various areas of pronunciation, and cover theory, factual knowledge and ideas for the classroom.

All the chapters except the first one contain a range of sample lessons which demonstrate Integrated, Remedial and Practice lesson types.

The Task File at the back of the book comprises a number of tasks relevant to each chapter. They can be used for individual study and reflection, or for discussion and revision in a training context. An answer key is provided where appropriate.

The appendices offer a newly designed learners' reference chart of English sounds, a summary of common pronunciation difficulties, a set of sound and spelling tables, and suggestions for further reading.

The Compact Disc accompanying the book contains examples of sounds and sentences from the text. The relevant CD track numbers are indicated within the book by the symbol on the left.

1 The description of speech

- **What are the main features of pronunciation?**
- **The physiology of pronunciation**
- **The articulation of phonemes**
- **Phonemic transcription**
- **Phonetics and phonology**

What are the main features of pronunciation?

In order to study how something works it is often useful to break it down into its constituent parts. The following diagram shows a breakdown of the main features of pronunciation.

Features of pronunciation

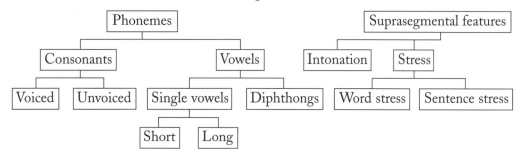

Phonemes

Phonemes are the different sounds within a language. Although there are slight differences in how individuals articulate sounds, we can still describe reasonably accurately how each sound is produced. When considering meaning, we see how using one sound rather than another can change the meaning of the word. It is this principle which gives us the total number of phonemes in a particular language. For example, the word *rat* has the phonemes /ræt/. (Refer to the **sounds chart** on the next page if you are not familiar with the symbols used here.) If we change the middle phoneme, we get /rɒt/ *rot*, a different word. If you or I pronounce /r/ in a slightly different way, the word doesn't change, and we still understand that we mean the same thing. To make an analogy, our individual perceptions of colours may theoretically vary (i.e. your notion of 'green' may not be the same as mine), but intuitively we know that we are likely to be thinking about more or less the same thing. We can both look at a green traffic light and understand its significance, and how it differs from a red one.

Sounds may be **voiced** or **unvoiced** (sometimes referred to as 'voiceless'). Voiced sounds occur when the vocal cords in the larynx are vibrated. It is easy to tell whether a sound is voiced or not by placing one or two fingers on your Adam's apple. If you are producing a voiced sound, you will feel vibration; if you are producing an unvoiced sound, you will not. The difference between /f/ and /v/, for example, can be heard by putting your top teeth on your bottom lip, breathing out in a continuous stream to produce /f/, then adding your voice to make /v/. Hold your Adam's apple while doing this, and you will feel the vibration.

The set of phonemes consists of two categories: **vowel** sounds and **consonant** sounds. However, these do not necessarily correspond to the vowels and consonants we are familiar with in the alphabet. Vowel sounds are all voiced, and may be single (like /e/, as in l*e*t), or a combination, involving a movement from one vowel sound to another (like /eɪ/, as in l*a*te); such combinations are known as **diphthongs**. An additional term used is **triphthongs** which describes the combination of three vowel sounds (like /aʊə/ in *our* or *power*). Single vowel sounds may be short (like /ɪ/, as in h*i*t) or long (like /iː/, as in h*ea*t). The symbol /ː/ denotes a long sound.

Consonant sounds may be voiced or unvoiced. It is possible to identify many pairs of consonants which are essentially the same except for the element of voicing (for example /f/, as in *fan*, and /v/, as in *van*). The following table lists English phonemes, giving an example of a word in which each appears.

Vowels		Diphthongs		Consonants			
iː	b*ea*d	eɪ	c*a*ke	p	*p*in	s	*s*ue
ɪ	h*i*t	ɔɪ	t*oy*	b	*b*in	z	*z*oo
ʊ	b*oo*k	aɪ	h*igh*	t	*t*o	ʃ	*sh*e
uː	f*oo*d	ɪə	b*eer*	d	*d*o	ʒ	mea*s*ure
e	l*e*ft	ʊə	f*ewe*r	k	*c*ot	h	*h*ello
ə	*a*bout	eə	*wh*ere	g	*g*ot	m	*m*ore
ɜː	sh*ir*t	əʊ	*go*	tʃ	*ch*ur*ch*	n	*n*o
ɔː	c*a*ll	aʊ	h*ou*se	dʒ	*j*u*dg*e	ŋ	si*ng*
æ	h*a*t			f	*f*an	l	*l*ive
ʌ	r*u*n			v	*v*an	r	*r*ed
ɑː	f*ar*			θ	*th*ink	j	*y*es
ɒ	d*o*g			ð	*th*e	w	*w*ood

(Pairs of consonants (voiced and unvoiced) are thickly outlined. The boxes containing unvoiced phonemes are shaded.)

Suprasegmental features

Phonemes, as we have seen, are units of sound which we can analyse. They are also known as **segments**. **Suprasegmental features**, as the name implies, are features of speech which generally apply to groups of segments, or phonemes. The features which are important in English are **stress**, **intonation**, and how sounds change in connected speech.

With regard to individual words, we can identify and teach word stress. Usually one syllable in a word will sound more prominent than the others, as in *PAper*, or *BOttle*. The stresses in words are usually indicated in dictionaries.

With regard to utterances, we can analyse and teach intonation as well as stress, although as features they can at times be quite hard to consciously recognise and to describe. Stress gives rhythm to speech. One or more words within each utterance are selected by the speaker as worthy of stressing, and thus made prominent to the listener. Intonation, on the other hand, is the way in which the **pitch** of the voice goes up and down in the course of an utterance. (When discussing speech the term **utterance** is used rather than 'sentence', as it refers to anything we say including grammatically incomplete sentences, and to different ways of saying the same sentence.)

Utterance stress and intonation patterns are often linked to the communication of meaning. For example, in the following utterance the speaker is asking a question for the first time. In this particular instance as you can hear on the CD, the pitch of her voice starts relatively high and falls at the end, finishing relatively low. This intonation pattern is shown here using an arrow.

(1)   Where do you live?

If the speaker should ask the question for a second time (having already been given the information, but having forgotten it), then the voice falls on the word *where* and rises again towards the end of the question. This indicates to the listener that the speaker is aware that they should know the answer.

(2)   Where do you live?

The next examples display how stress can have an equally significant role to play in the communication of meaning. The most stressed syllables within the utterances are in capitals. Changes to which syllable is stressed in the same sentence changes the meaning of the utterance in various subtle ways. The implied meaning is given in brackets after each utterance.

(3)   I'd like a cup of herbal TEA.   (A simple request.)
      I'd like a cup of HERbal tea.   (Not any other sort of tea.)
      I'd like a CUP of herbal tea.   (Not a mug.)

The first example is like the default choice, a first time request, while in the other two examples there is an apparent attempt to clear up some misunderstanding between the speaker and the listener. On the CD, we can notice how the speaker's voice falls on the syllables which are in capitals, demonstrating how intonation and stress are strongly linked in utterances.

The physiology of pronunciation

Teachers also need to consider how the sounds we use come about, and to study the physiology which allows us to use those sounds. We all use the same speech organs to produce the sounds we become accustomed to producing. The set of sounds we acquire, however, may vary: a child brought up in an English-speaking environment will develop the phonemes of English, a French-speaking child will develop a different set, and so on. We also learn to use our voices in different ways: the English-speaking child will learn to use appropriate stress and intonation patterns, and the Cantonese-speaking child will learn to use **tones** (see page 87) to give distinct meanings to the same set of sounds.

To a certain extent we can learn to use our speech organs in new ways in order to produce learnt sounds in a foreign language, or to lose sounds from our own language which are not appropriate in the foreign language. It seems, however, that after childhood our ability to adopt an unfamiliar set of sounds diminishes somewhat.

The diagram below shows the location of the main areas of the head and neck associated with the production of sounds. In the human larynx (or 'voice box', as it is commonly known), there are two flaps of elastic, connective tissue known as vocal cords, which can open and close. During normal breathing, and also in the production of **unvoiced** sounds, the cords are open. When the edges of the vocal cords come close together, the air which passes between them makes them vibrate, resulting in **voicing**. The **pitch** of the sound (how high or low) is controlled by muscles which slacken and lengthen the cords for low tones, and shorten the cords, pulling them taut, for high-pitched tones.

We speak using the lips, tongue, teeth, hard and soft palates and alveolar ridge. (See the diagram below.) The nasal cavity comes into play for certain sounds, and the movement of the lower jaw is also important. Articulation happens when the airstream is interrupted, shaped, restricted or diverted. The role played by each physiological feature in the articulation of vowels and consonants is summarised in this chapter, and there is a more detailed investigation of the articulation of individual phonemes in Chapters 3 and 4.

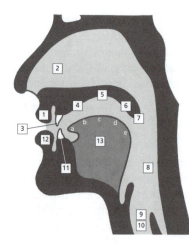

1 Upper lip	10 Larynx
2 Nasal cavity	11 Lower teeth
3 Upper teeth	12 Lower lip
4 Alveolar ridge	13 Tongue
5 Hard palate	a tip
6 Soft palate	b blade
7 Uvula	c front
8 Pharynx	d centre
9 Glottis	e back

The articulation of phonemes

The articulation of vowels

Vowels are produced when the airstream is voiced through the vibration of the vocal cords in the larynx, and then shaped using the tongue and the lips to modify the overall shape of the mouth. The position of the tongue is a useful reference point for describing the differences between vowel sounds, and these are summarised in the following diagram.

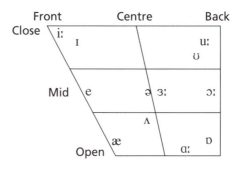

The diagram is a representation of the 'vowel space' in the centre of the mouth where vowel sounds are articulated.

- 'Close', 'Mid' and 'Open' refer to the distance between the tongue and the roof of the mouth.
- 'Front', 'Centre' and 'Back' and their corresponding 'vertical' lines refer to the part of the tongue.
- The position of each phoneme represents the height of the tongue, and also the part of the tongue which is (however relatively) raised.

Putting these together:

/iː/ *bead* (a close front vowel) is produced when the front of the tongue is the highest part, and is near the roof of the mouth.

/æ/ *hat* (an open front vowel) is produced when the front of the tongue is the highest part, but the tongue itself is low in the mouth.

/ɒ/ *dog* (an open back vowel) is produced when the back of the tongue is the highest part, but the tongue itself is low in the mouth.

/uː/ *food* (a close back vowel) is produced when the back of the tongue is the highest part, and is near the roof of the mouth.

The articulation of consonants

Consonants, as mentioned earlier, can be voiced or unvoiced. The articulation of /p/ or /b/ is effectively the same, the only difference being that the latter is voiced and the former is unvoiced. As the relative force involved in producing /p/ is greater than that used to produce /b/, the terms **fortis** (strong) and **lenis** (weak) are sometimes used. Try holding a small slip of paper in front of your mouth and making both sounds; the paper should flap for /p/ and hardly move for /b/. Essentially, in English at least, 'fortis' applies to unvoiced consonant sounds like /p/, whereas 'lenis' describes their voiced counterparts like /b/. In addition to the presence or absence of voicing, consonants can be described in terms of the **manner** and **place of articulation**.

With regard to the manner of articulation, the vocal tract may be completely closed so that the air is temporarily unable to pass through. Alternatively there may be a closing movement of the lips, tongue or throat, so that it is possible to hear the sound made by air passing through. Or, as in the case of nasal sounds, the air is diverted through the nasal passages. The various terms used are explained in the following table:

Manner of articulation	
plosive	a complete closure is made somewhere in the vocal tract, and the soft palate is also raised. Air pressure increases behind the closure, and is then released 'explosively', e.g. /p/ and /b/
affricate	a complete closure is made somewhere in the mouth, and the soft palate is raised. Air pressure increases behind the closure, and is then released more slowly than in plosives, e.g. /tʃ/ and /dʒ/
fricative	when two vocal organs come close enough together for the movement of air between them to be heard, e.g. /f/ and /v/
nasal	a closure is made by the lips, or by the tongue against the palate, the soft palate is lowered, and air escapes through the nose, e.g. /m/ and /n/
lateral	a partial closure is made by the blade of the tongue against the alveolar ridge. Air is able to flow around the sides of the tongue, e.g. /l/
approximant	vocal organs come near to each other, but not so close as to cause audible friction, e.g. /r/ and /w/

With regard to the place of articulation, the following table summarises the main movements of the various articulators:

Place of articulation	
bilabial	using closing movement of both lips, e.g. /p/ and /m/
labio-dental	using the lower lip and the upper teeth, e.g. /f/ and /v/
dental	the tongue tip is used either between the teeth or close to the upper teeth, e.g. /θ/ and /ð/
alveolar	the blade of the tongue is used close to the alveolar ridge, e.g. /t/ and /s/
palato-alveolar	the blade (or tip) of the tongue is used just behind the alveolar ridge, e.g. /tʃ/ and /dʒ/
palatal	the front of the tongue is raised close to the palate, e.g. /j/
velar	the back of the tongue is used against the soft palate, e.g. /k/ and /ŋ/
glottal	the gap between the vocal cords is used to make audible friction, e.g. /h/

Voicing, manner and place of articulation are together summarised in the following table:

Table of English Consonant Phonemes									
		Place of articulation							
		Front ─────────────────────────────→ Back							
		bilabial	labio-dental	dental	alveolar	palato-alveolar	palatal	velar	glottal
Manner of articulation	plosive	p b			t d			k g	
	affricate					tʃ dʒ			
	fricative		f v	θ ð	s z	ʃ ʒ			h
	nasal	m			n			ŋ	
	lateral				l				
	approxi-mant	(w)					r	j	w

(Unvoiced phonemes are on a shaded background. Voiced phonemes are on a white background.)

Phonemic transcription

When writing in English, we use 5 vowel and 21 consonant letters. When speaking English we typically use 20 different vowel sounds (including 12 diphthongs), and 24 consonant sounds.

In some languages, there is essentially a one-to-one relationship between spelling and pronunciation, and there will be (with the occasional exception) the same number of phonemes used in the language as there are letters in the alphabet.

The lack of a one-to-one relationship between spelling and pronunciation in English, while by no means being unique, presents learners with many problems. A typically cited example is the pronunciation of *ough*, which has at least eight distinct sound patterns attached to it:

cough /kɒf/	through /θruː/
bough /baʊ/	bought /bɔːt/
rough /rʌf/	thorough /ˈθʌrə/*
although /ɔːlˈðəʊ/	lough /lɒx/**

* British English. /ˈθʌrəʊ/ is more common in US English.
** /x/ represents the same sound as at the end of the more familiar 'loch'; the spelling used depends upon the variety of English.

Examples abound of spellings and pronunciations which can cause difficulties for learners:

Why don't you read /riːd/ this book?
Oh, I've already read /red/ it.
Look over there! I can see /siː/ the sea /siː/.

The difficulties that individual learners have may stem from one or more of the following:

- The learner's first language (referred to as **L1**) may have a one-to-one relationship between sounds and spelling. The concept of there not being such a relationship may be new.
- Even if such a concept is not new for the learner, they will have to become familiar with new sound–spelling relationships.
- There may be sounds, and combinations of sounds in L1, which do not occur in English.
- There may be sounds, and combinations of sounds, used in English which do not occur in L1.
- English may use stress and intonation patterns which feel strange to the learner.

Phonemic transcription gives both teachers and students a way of accurately recording the pronunciations of words and utterances.

It is not suggested that teachers should introduce their students to all of the phonemic symbols at once. It makes far more sense to work on those sounds which cause difficulty first, and introduce other phonemic symbols as appropriate. It is possible to tie in the teaching of new symbols with dictionary work, when the teacher can show students how the symbols are used. Be aware, though, that dictionaries may vary in the conventions they use. The best advice is to use a class set of the dictionary you or your students have chosen, and familiarise students with the conventions it uses.

The following examples are used to show certain conventions used in this book, and found in most dictionaries and reference books. It is useful for teachers to know these conventions, and to help students become familiar with them to aid independent study away from the classroom.

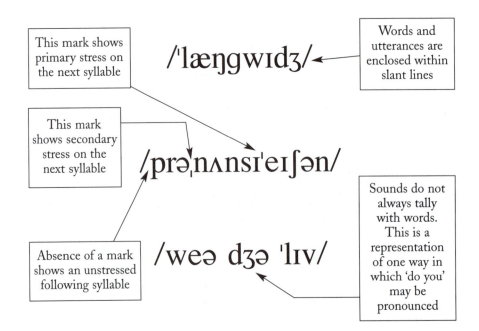

This mark shows primary stress on the next syllable

Words and utterances are enclosed within slant lines

/ˈlæŋgwɪdʒ/

This mark shows secondary stress on the next syllable

/prəˌnʌnsɪˈeɪʃən/

Absence of a mark shows an unstressed following syllable

Sounds do not always tally with words. This is a representation of one way in which 'do you' may be pronounced

/weə dʒə ˈlɪv/

Other conventions exist for marking stress and intonation, which may be easier for students to understand. Chapters 5 and 6 will explain the theory behind their use and will also show teachers how to incorporate both standard and alternative notations for indicating stress and intonation in transcription. As suggested above, dictionary work can be very useful, not only because it helps foster independence in the learner, but also because learners will get used to seeing stress symbols used in the word transcriptions.

Phonetics and phonology

The study of pronunciation consists of two fields, namely **phonetics** and **phonology**. Phonetics refers to the study of speech sounds. A phonetician usually works in one or more of the following areas:

- the anatomical, neurological and physiological bases of speech (collectively known as **physiological phonetics**)
- the actions and movements of the speech organs in producing sounds (**articulatory phonetics**)
- the nature and acoustics of the sound waves which transmit speech (**acoustic phonetics**)
- how speech is received by the ears (**auditory phonetics**)
- how speech is perceived by the brain (**perceptual phonetics**)

Phonetics is a wide-ranging field, and it does not necessarily have a direct connection with the study of language itself. While the phonetic disciplines listed above can be studied independently of one another, they are clearly connected: speech organs move to produce sounds, which travel in sound waves, which are received by the ears and transmitted to the brain.

If phonetics deals with the physical reality of speech sounds, then **phonology**, on the other hand, is primarily concerned with how we interpret and systematise sounds. Phonology deals with the system and pattern of the sounds which exist within particular languages. The study of the phonology of English looks at the **vowels**, **consonants** and **suprasegmental** features of the language. Within the discipline of phonology, when we talk about vowels and consonants we are referring to the different sounds we make when speaking, and not the vowel and consonant letters we refer to when talking about spelling. It would be wrong to assume that phonology is always monolingual. Much work in phonological study deals with generalisations concerning the organisation and interpretation of sounds that might apply across different languages.

This book, while being primarily concerned with the phonology of English and how it might be integrated successfully into language teaching, will also draw on aspects of phonetics, particularly those concerned with articulation. As we will see, both fields have practical significance and application in the classroom.

Conclusions   In this chapter we have:
- introduced the main features of pronunciation, and distinguished between phonemes and suprasegmental features.
- introduced the vowel sounds. Vowel sounds are usually described in terms of the tongue position, which may be shown diagrammatically.
- introduced the consonant sounds. Consonant sounds are formed when the airflow is interrupted, restricted or diverted in a variety of ways.
- considered stress and intonation. Stress is described in terms of the prominences made in words and utterances. Intonation is described in terms of how the voice goes up or down across utterances.
- thought about reasons for using phonemic transcription in the classroom, as a way of accurately noting pronunciation and shown how transcription can be used to show sounds, stresses and intonation.
- distinguished between phonetics and phonology, and suggested that both areas have practical significance for teachers.

Looking ahead   In Chapter 2 we will:
- look closely at various ways of dealing with pronunciation in the classroom, and exemplify three different types of pronunciation lesson.

2 Teaching pronunciation

- Why teach pronunciation?
- Problems and approaches in pronunciation teaching
- What pronunciation model to teach
- Techniques and activities
- Sample lessons
    - Lesson 1: 'Alice': Planning an Integrated lesson
    - Lesson 2: Organising a party: Remedial lessons
    - Lesson 3: Minimal pairs: A Practice lesson

Why teach pronunciation? A consideration of learners' pronunciation errors and of how these can inhibit successful communication is a useful basis on which to assess why it is important to deal with pronunciation in the classroom. When a learner says, for example, *soap* in a situation such as a restaurant where they should have said *soup*, the inaccurate production of a phoneme can lead to misunderstanding (at least on the part of the waitress). A learner who consistently mispronounces a range of phonemes can be extremely difficult for a speaker from another language community to understand. This can be very frustrating for the learner who may have a good command of grammar and lexis but have difficulty in understanding and being understood by a native speaker.

The inaccurate use of suprasegmental elements, such as stress or intonation, can also cause problems. For example, the following request was made by a Turkish learner in a classroom:

(4)   Do you mind if I Open the window?

Notice how the sentence stress is on the /əʊ/ of *open*. As it was a first request, one might have expected the first syllable of *window* to have been the most prominent, rather than the first syllable of *open*. Had the teacher not known better, the utterance could have been interpreted as being a second request (the first request perhaps not having been heard), and possibly being uttered with some impatience. In short, it could appear rude.

11

The intonation pattern used in the following question caused the listener to misunderstand it.

(5) How long have you been in London?

This example was spoken by an Italian learner, as a 'getting to know you' question to a new friend. The unexpected fall of her voice on *been* led to the friend not understanding her question. (One would expect the voice to fall on the first syllable of *London*). She had to repeat the question before making herself understood.

Intonation and stress can also indicate the **function** of an utterance. The function of an utterance is what it is being used for. For example, the following sentence has the function of a 'request':

Can you help me, please?

Now consider this sentence:

(6) a) Why don't you come to my PARty?

As a first 'suggestion' or 'invitation', we might expect the first syllable of *party* to be stressed, as indicated with capitals, and we might expect the voice to go down at the end, as shown by the arrow. Now consider this variation:

(7) b) WHY don't you come to my party?

When spoken in this way the question is no longer a simple invitation. It suggests instead that someone has refused the invitation and that the speaker is upset by this and needs to know why it has happened. If a student uses this stress and intonation for a straightforward invitation rather than speaking as in example (a), it is possible that there will be a misunderstanding.

The above examples all show problems caused by pronunciation errors which led to a problem of **reception**, or comprehension of the meaning or function of an utterance. But pronunciation can also affect the perceived tone or mood of an utterance. Aspects of a student's first language can interfere with the pronunciation of a second language not only in terms of accent but also in terms of mood. For example, features of certain German accents may lead to German people sounding, completely unintentionally, abrupt or impolite when speaking in English. Spanish speakers tend to use a narrower range of intonation than L1 English speakers, and as a result may sometimes sound rather bored to a native speaker. Even though these difficulties are subtle, they are very real, and worthy of investigation and remedial action in the classroom.

Not all pronunciation difficulties necessarily get in the way of communication, of course. If a German student wants to ask permission to open a window, for example, if she pronounces *window* as /'vɪndəʊ/ it is unlikely to get in the way of the message. Teachers, therefore, need to prioritise, and not correct everything. It is, however, important to recognise that even if students are not having difficulties communicating, they often like to have their pronunciation mistakes brought to their attention.

Problems and approaches in pronunciation teaching

There are two key problems with pronunciation teaching. Firstly it tends to be neglected. And secondly when it is not neglected, it tends to be reactive to a particular problem that has arisen in the classroom rather than being strategically planned.

A paradox

The fact that pronunciation tends to suffer from neglect may not be due to teachers lacking interest in the subject but rather to a feeling of doubt as to how to teach it. Many experienced teachers would admit to a lack of knowledge of the theory of pronunciation and they may therefore feel the need to improve their practical skills in pronunciation teaching. In spite of the fact that trainees and less experienced teachers may be very interested in pronunciation, their concern with grammar and vocabulary tends to take precedence. Language learners, on the other hand, often show considerable enthusiasm for pronunciation. They feel it is something that would help them to communicate better. So, paradoxically, even though both teachers and learners are keen on the subject, it is often neglected.

Teachers of pronunciation need:

- a good grounding in theoretical knowledge
- practical classroom skills
- access to good ideas for classroom activities

From reactive to planned teaching

A lot of pronunciation teaching tends to be done in response to errors which students make in the classroom. Such reactive teaching is, of course, absolutely necessary, and will always be so. Grammatical and lexical difficulties arise in the classroom too, and teachers also deal with these reactively. However, when it comes to planning a lesson or devising a timetable of work to be covered, teachers tend to make grammar their first concern. Lexis follows closely behind, with items of vocabulary and longer phrases being 'slotted in' where appropriate. A look at the contents pages of most coursebooks will show that we tend to think of the organisation of language in terms of grammatical structures, although some more recent publications claim to have a lexically arranged syllabus. Therefore, it is quite natural to make grammar the primary reference when planning lessons.

Yet pronunciation work can, and should, be planned for too. Teachers should regard features of pronunciation as integral to language analysis and lesson planning. Any analysis of language that disregards or sidelines factors of pronunciation is incomplete. Similarly, a lesson which focuses on particular language structures or lexis needs to include features of pronunciation in order to give students the full picture, and hence a better chance of being able to communicate successfully. While planning, teachers should decide what pronunciation issues are relevant to the particular structures and lexis being dealt with in the lesson. They can also anticipate the pronunciation difficulties their students are likely to experience, and further plan their lessons accordingly. There will still, of course, be reactive work to be done in the classroom, just as there is with grammar and lexis, but by anticipating and planning, the teacher can present a fuller analysis to learners, and give them the opportunity for fuller language practice. Integrating pronunciation teaching fully with the study of grammatical and lexical features has the further incremental benefit that learners will increasingly appreciate the significance of pronunciation in determining successful communication.

In the light of this and throughout this book, sample lessons are divided into three main types:

- **Integrated** lessons, in which pronunciation forms an essential part of the language analysis and the planning process, and the language presentation and practice within the lesson.

- **Remedial** or reactive lessons, where a pronunciation difficulty which arises in class is dealt with there and then, in order to facilitate the successful achievement of classroom tasks.

- **Practice** lessons, in which a particular feature of pronunciation is isolated and practised for its own sake, forming the main focus of a lesson period.

What pronunciation model to teach

English long ago outgrew the limits of the land from which it takes its name. If we compare the languages of countries or regions where it is used as a first language, we can see that it has changed significantly. One need only think about the varieties of English used in Britain, Ireland, the USA, Australia and Canada. As the use of English spreads further in countries where it is not the first language, such development continues with ever new varieties of English emerging. The growth in the use of English, together with the ease of communication worldwide, means that English is increasingly being used as a medium of communication between speakers for whom it is not a first language.

This can raise both theoretical and practical issues for teachers. There can be disagreement over the **model** of English one should provide for one's students. The term 'model' here is used to refer to the pronunciation characteristics of the language a teacher presents to learners in the classroom.

In the past the preferred pronunciation model for teaching in Britain, or among British teachers abroad, was **Received Pronunciation** (or RP). There are many different accents within the variety known as British English, and most of these give some clue as to the regional origins of the speaker. RP is different, in that it says more about social standing than geography. It is still perceived as signifying status and education, and 'the Queen's English', or 'BBC English' are often used as synonyms. The accent was first described as 'Received Pronunciation' by dialectologist A. J. Ellis, in 1869. However, the number of people who speak with an RP accent in Britain is currently estimated at about only 3% of the population and declining. It is also falling out of favour as a teaching model because few British teachers naturally speak with this accent. However, RP has been the basis of much modern investigation into pronunciation and so its influence persists.

As a teacher the model one uses in the classroom will usually be close to the language one uses outside the classroom. Many teachers modify their accent slightly for the benefit of their students, but few could consistently teach with an accent significantly different from their own, even if they wanted to. However, language teachers need to be aware of variations and differences, and the more knowledge one has with regard to different accents and varieties of English, the more informed one's teaching is likely to be.

As ever, it is important to consider the needs of learners. For many, RP is still the target for pronunciation, because of its traditional status, though this is slowly changing. Learners will usually have a target model in mind, whether this be British, American, Irish, Australian or any other variety of English. Targets tend to be highly personal, and on occasion rather vague. They may also vary within a class where learners aiming for British English are seated alongside others aiming for American English (perhaps because of the people they meet or work with outside the classroom). And if the teacher is Australian, what model can and should she provide? This may be a theoretical situation but, particularly in multilingual classes, one finds students who have already been taught by teachers with different accents and varieties of English. In monolingual classes too, one finds a range of personal targets for pronunciation.

There are no easy answers here, though teachers can, in catering for their students' needs, work on issues of **production** and **reception** independently, enabling students to understand a wide range of varieties, while allowing them to choose their own target model so long as it is widely comprehensible. In work on reception, teachers can, for example, focus on vowel differences between British and American English, or the rising intonation of Australian utterances in contrast to the way such utterances are completed by speakers of other English varieties. The best advice for teachers is to teach what they know and use, and be as informed as they can be about other varieties.

Techniques and activities

Once having decided to make pronunciation an integral part of their teaching, and adopted a policy on models, what techniques and activities can teachers employ? The range is multifarious from highly focused techniques, such as drilling, to more broad-reaching activities such as getting students to notice (look out for) particular pronunciation features within listening texts. Furthermore, as indicated above, there are two key sides to pronunciation teaching – namely, the teaching of **productive** skills on the one hand and the teaching of **receptive** skills on the other. In terms of reception, students need to learn to hear the difference between phonemes, for example, particularly where such a contrast does not exist in their L1. They then need to carry that knowledge through into their production. Drills, by way of example, are useful in the development of both kinds of skill, while noticing tasks used with listening texts will be most effective in the development of receptive skills.

Drilling

One of the main ways in which pronunciation is practised in the classroom is through drilling. In its most basic form, drilling simply involves the teacher saying a word or structure, and getting the class to repeat it. Being able to drill properly is a basic and fundamental language teaching skill. The technique has its roots in behaviourist psychological theory and 'audio-lingual' approaches to teaching; these are both now largely consigned to history, though drilling has stayed with us as a tried and tested classroom technique. Drilling aims to help students achieve better pronunciation of language items, and to help them remember new items. This is a crucial part of classroom pronunciation work, and is possibly the time in the lesson when students are most reliant on the teacher.

Drilling often follows on from the process, known as **eliciting**, of encouraging students to bring up a previously studied word, phrase or structure. The teacher generally uses prompts, pictures, mime etc, to help the process along, and can give the relevant item to the students if none of them is able to offer it. Given the complex relationships between English spelling and pronunciation, drilling is best done before students see the written form of the language. Once the item in question has arisen, teachers can then drill it in order to work on pronunciation. The teacher's main role in drilling is that of providing a model of the word, phrase or structure for the students to copy. You can hear an example of drilling on the CD. Teachers generally drill 'chorally' first of all, which means inviting the whole class to repeat the item in unison. Choral drilling can help to build confidence, and gives students the chance to practise pronouncing the drilled item relatively anonymously, without being put on the spot. It is typically followed by individual drilling, where students are invited one-by-one to repeat. This gives the teacher the chance to ascertain how well individuals are able to pronounce the item being drilled. Teachers usually select individuals more or less at random; doing so is seen to help keep students on their toes.

Chaining can be used for sentences which prove difficult for students to pronounce, either because they are long, or because they include difficult words and sounds. The following examples show how the teacher isolates certain parts of the sentence, modelling them separately for students to repeat, and gradually building the sentence up until it is complete.

Back chain

The sentence is drilled and built up from the end, gradually adding to its length. Certain parts may be drilled separately, if they present problems. Each part of the sentence is modelled by the teacher, and the students repeat.

...told him.
...would've...
...would've told...
I would've told him.
If I'd seen him...
If I'd seen him, I would've told him.

> **Front chain**
> The sentence is drilled and built up from the start, gradually adding to its length. Certain parts may be drilled separately, if they present problems. Each part of the sentence is modelled by the teacher, and the students repeat.
>
> If I'd seen him...
> If I'd seen him, I would've...
> I would've...
> I would've told him.
> If I'd seen him, I would've told him.

Another common variation is **'open pair' drilling**, where, for example, question and answer drills might be set up across the class, with one student (S) asking, another responding, and so on. Having drilled a question and answer chorally and individually, the teacher (T) uses prompts (for example a big letter 'Q' and a big letter 'A' written on cards) and invites students to question each other and respond in turn across the class, as shown in the following diagram.

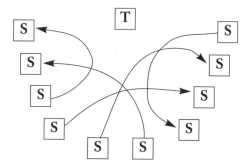

The resulting question and answer routine might then sound like this:

Student 1:   Have you ever been to Paris?
Student 4:   Yes, I have.
Student 5:   Have you ever been to New York?
Student 2:   No, I haven't.
etc.

Substitution drilling is another important and useful variation. This involves drilling a structure, but substituting items of vocabulary into the sentence being dealt with, as follows:

Teacher: It's in the corner.
Student 1:   It's in the corner.
Teacher: It's on the table.
Student 2:   It's on the table.
Teacher: It's under the chair.
etc.

Drilling is also fundamental to the teaching of word stress, sentence stress and intonation. Teachers should aim to model utterances as naturally as possible, according to the context in which the language is being used. Bear in mind that slight changes in stress and intonation can have a significant impact on meaning and appropriacy, as discussed earlier in this chapter. Teachers often beat out the rhythm of the stress pattern while drilling. Some teachers beat the air with their finger, some click their fingers, some tap on a surface; teachers should choose whatever comes naturally to them, and then use the same method consistently.

Drilling is an important tool in pronunciation work. Many teachers skimp on drilling because they feel that it is something that only needs to be done at lower levels, yet it is important at higher levels too. As students will spend a lot of time adding new words and phrases to their vocabulary, they will need to be sure of how to say them.

Minimal pairs and related activities

In Chapter 1, the examples *rat* /ræt/ and *rot* /rɒt/ were used to show the phonemic principle in action; changing just one sound leads to a change in meaning. The same applies to words like *soap* /səʊp/ and *soup* /suːp/, and *paper* /'peɪpə/ and *pepper* /'pepə/.

These are all examples of minimal pairs – words or utterances which differ by only one phoneme. Teachers can use minimal pairs to good advantage in the classroom as a way of focusing on sounds which have been causing difficulties for students. Here is an example for Spanish and Italian speakers:

Words	Sounds	Useful for...(e.g.)	Because...
cat /kæt/ cut /kʌt/	/æ/ /ʌ/	Spanish	/æ/ /ʌ/ and /ɑː/ correspond roughly to one sound /a/ in Spanish
		Italian	/ʌ/ is often produced as /æ/

The 'because' column is very important here. There seems little advantage in practising sounds which do not cause problems for students, except to reinforce a point recently made or investigated in class. In a monolingual class the teacher can practise sounds that are likely to cause problems for their students, but would do better, as mentioned above, to concentrate on sounds which actually do. The same applies to a multilingual class. In this context the possible number of pronunciation difficulties is bigger, but it may be frustrating for students who do not have a problem with the difference between /æ/ and /ʌ/ or /ɔː/ and /ɒ/, for example, to spend classroom time practising them.

But if half of a multilingual class do have a problem, then something needs to be done. One useful idea is multilingual peer teaching, where students help each other to work on particular sounds. This works more successfully if everyone has something they can teach to their peers, and so some planning and research is required on the part of the teacher to ensure a balance of everyone getting about as much help as they give, as far as is reasonably possible. Smaller, monolingual groups can be set up initially so that the teacher can provide some coaching. Individuals can be coached too.

Some ideas for activities based around minimal pairs are as follows:

1. Students can be given lists of words and work with a partner to decide which words have a particular sound:

> **Tick the words which have the sound /ʌ/:**
>
> cap   hat   bug   cup   hut   bag

Activities like this one are a good way of gradually introducing students to the individual phonemic symbols relevant to English. Other potentially 'conflicting' sounds can be introduced too, such as the following 'minimal trio':

> hat   heart   hut

2. Students might also listen to a succession of words, and decide how many times a particular sound is heard:

> **How many times do you hear /eɪ/?**
> **Underline each one you hear.**
>
> pepper   paper   letter   later   pen   pain
> wet   wait   get   gate   late   let

3. Sounds can also be contrasted by appearing in close proximity. The teacher can drill these utterances chorally and individually:

> Pass me the pepper and the paper.
> I'll post the letter later.
> They won't let us in if we're late.

4. In a similar vein, but moving slightly away from the idea of minimal pairs, teachers can also ask students to listen for the odd one out among a list of words that they are given:

> cart   class   heart   learn   smart   part

Although there is no shortage of variations for teachers to experiment with, the difficulty with minimal pairs exercises is that one can end up using words which are unknown to the students, and which are hence less meaningful. Fairly often used pairings such as *hag* and *hug*, *bag* and *bug*, while practising the sounds that the teacher wants to see practised, are of limited use if students don't know what a *hag* or a *bug* is, or are unlikely to have to use these words. The teacher can always teach them, of course, but this might not always be the wisest use of classroom time. It can be more useful to choose words which are recent or current in the students' learning experience, in order to show the sound in its context. If there happen to be minimal pairs available, they certainly provide a useful opportunity for focusing just on the sound in question. If not, then focusing solely on known words can at times be more productive than introducing new words simply for the sake of a minimal pairs exercise. What one loses on the *hag*, one gains on the *hug*, so to speak.

Rather than using words provided by the teacher, it can also make more sense to use the students' active vocabulary in order to practise sounds. Students can be asked to provide (or suggest) their own minimal pairs to try out on their peers.

Pronunciation and spelling activities

It makes sense to tie pronunciation work closely in with spelling work, in order to investigate the different ways in which sounds can be represented on the page. Chapter 8 looks in detail at the relationships between pronunciation and spelling, but some basic ideas are outlined here.

Homographs and **homophones** can provide useful opportunities for such work. Homographs are words which have the same spelling, but with different pronunciations (*Why don't you read this book?* and *I've already read it*; *wind* /wɪnd/ as in weather, and *wind* /waɪnd/ as in what you do to a clock). Homophones are words which have the same pronunciation, but have different spellings (*write* and *right*; *there*, *their* and *they're*; *fair* and *fare*).

These may be used as the basis of many types of activity, such as when, in the case of homophones, students listen to a sentence and have to choose which from a printed list of words in front of them is the word with the correct spelling for a particular word they heard in the sentence. Classroom work can also be done which concentrates on the properties or effects of particular letters when they appear in words. For example, in a discovery type exercise, students can study pairs of words, like the ones below, and work out a rule for how the vowel sound changes when the letter *e* is added:

hat hate   kit kite   cut cute

In each instance, the answer is something like: adding the *e* makes the vowel (e.g. /æ/) sound like the name of that vowel in the alphabet (e.g. *A*).

Tendencies like these above can be used in discrimination exercises, dictated, introduced in listening or reading exercises, elicited and drilled, dealt with through crosswords, board games, etc. Teachers need to decide what is relevant to their class at a particular time.

Taping students' English

Taping learners' spoken English from time to time can pay dividends. Tapes can be made while students are engaged in language practice activities, and used for all manner of language difficulties, but especially those concerned with pronunciation. If the teacher is sufficiently prepared, tapes of the completion of whole tasks can be contrasted with, for example, a group of native speakers or a higher level group of students tackling an identical task. Alternatively, students might tackle the same task on two occasions, the tape of the first 'attempt' providing the basis for pronunciation work; the subsequent performance of the task will (hopefully) be more successful, and the two attempts can then be contrasted.

Individual students can also be taped, particularly if they have a 'lingering' pronunciation difficulty which proves difficult to shake off. Sounds, stress and intonation can be contrasted with those of a native speaker, other students, or a fellow L1 speaker who doesn't have the same difficulty.

Listening activities

The anticipated outcome of language teaching is for students to be more able to understand and use the language outside the classroom. Many classroom activities therefore aim to reproduce, as far as possible, the authenticity of day-to-day communication. While authentic materials (i.e. printed, broadcast or taped material not produced with the classroom in mind) are valuable, it is impractical for teachers to use such material all the time, as one not only has to find suitable materials, but also design tasks to go with them.

Listening comprehension exercises in coursebooks are often designed to sound as realistic as possible, with the participants talking at a normal speed and using natural language. These can play a key role in helping students to notice the existence of a pronunciation feature.

For example, prior to doing a listening task, students can have the meaning and the pronunciation of a particular aspect of language brought to their attention, and practise it in very controlled ways. The particular issue may be the structural and pronunciation characteristics of the third person present simple or, at a higher level, of the third conditional (*I'd've gone if I'd known*). The listening exercise can then require students to listen out for this area of language and listen out for how it is used and pronounced in the context of a narrative or, say, a conversation.

Alternatively, an extended listening stage can precede an eliciting and drilling stage. Indeed it can be argued that putting the listening exercise first might even make the pronunciation elements of the lesson more of an issue with regard to comprehension, and more likely to be noticed by the students. Students would initially have to listen out for and interpret the use of the language and related pronunciation areas selected for study, in order to complete a set of tasks; work on the pronunciation and use of the language area in question could then follow on from the listening exercise.

Either way, a teacher's choice here would be informed by his or her knowledge of the students, their language skills, and how well he or she feels they would be able to perform the various tasks. Whatever order is chosen, the combination of pronunciation study with listening activities involves getting students to notice things about the language and its use. The concept of **noticing** is important in pronunciation work. A language item needs to be relevant to the student at a particular time in order for there to be conscious intake and before the student can use it consistently. The same applies to features of pronunciation. Language teaching attempts to help students to notice language, by making particular aspects or items of language relevant. Noticing is not only of relevance to the initial presentation of an item but is also of use in the recycling of items. Language always needs to be revised and recycled, as there is no guarantee that the features dealt with in a first presentation will be successfully remembered and used.

Reading activities

In reading activities, although the medium is the written word, work on pronunciation can be successfully integrated here too. Like listening, reading is a receptive activity (i.e. students receive the language rather than produce it), and so it provides a suitable means of bringing language features to students' attention.

Many teachers stage reading activities either by having an initial exercise to allow students to get the gist of the text they are reading, or by establishing the type of text being used, followed by some more detailed work to focus on specific details when the text is read again. At some stage, when a text is read aloud either by the teacher or the students, pronunciation work can be integrated. Such texts as poems, rhymes, extracts from plays, song lyrics etc. can be used creatively in the classroom and can offer plenty of scope for pronunciation work. Depending on preference, anything from Shakespeare to Dr Seuss, from Longfellow to limericks can be used to good advantage.

Reading aloud is a classroom activity which has fallen in and out of favour with teachers at various times. The main argument against it is that it can interfere with successful pronunciation; spellings can clearly affect pronunciation performance adversely. But reading aloud offers opportunities for the study of the links between spelling and pronunciation, of stress and intonation, and of the linking of sounds between words in connected speech; all of these can be highlighted and investigated further in fun and interesting ways through reading aloud.

Teachers need, however, to be clear as to the appropriacy of a text for pronunciation work. Reading aloud encyclopaedia texts, for example, might lead to a rather mechanical and monotone recitation of the words.

A final thought on pronunciation activities is that it is important to make sure that some are light-hearted. A fun way of practising the production of difficult sounds is through the use of tongue-twisters and rhymes. Most readers will be familiar with things like *Around the rugged rock the ragged rascal ran* (the problem sound here is fairly easy to ascertain!), and *She sells sea shells on the seashore...*

Sample lessons Here are three sample lessons, using a range of activities and techniques, and exemplifying the three types of pronunciation lesson discussed earlier: Integrated, Remedial, and Practice. The word 'lesson' is used here not necessarily to indicate a complete lesson period, though it probably does in the case of an Integrated or Practice lesson, but also to include a 'mini-lesson' or lessons within a classroom period as is likely to be the case with a Remedial lesson.

As we have discussed, pronunciation issues need to be made integral to lesson planning. The following explanation and lesson plan show an example of an Integrated lesson, which revises simple past tense verbs, and covers the activities of Alice on a night out in town. The first part of the plan gives an overview of the lesson, and the next part gives procedural detail.

Lesson 1: 'Alice': Planning an Integrated lesson (Intermediate)

Lesson type: Integrated
Materials: Taped listening, map, pictures for eliciting, picture story

In the pronunciation of regular past tense endings, the words *walked*, *lived* and *started* all have *-ed* at the end, but all have different pronunciations (/t/, /d/ and /ɪd/ respectively). Problems which students may have with these will often become apparent when the teacher is dealing with regular past tenses or past participles. There are some 'rules' here which can be given to students in order to help them generate further examples:

> *-ed* is pronounced as /t/ after most unvoiced consonants like /k/, as /d/ after most voiced consonants like /v/, and as /ɪd/ after /t/ or /d/. Also, if a verb ends in *-y* (as in *hurry*, *worry* or *marry*), the simple past form will end in *-ied*, and the pronunciation can be /iːd/ or /ɪd/, according to personal preference or habit.

In practice, the physical difficulty of pronouncing *-ed* as /d/ after an unvoiced consonant means that the incorrect use of /d/ instead of /t/ is seldom a pronunciation problem. What does tend to happen is that many students are tempted to insert the vowel sound /e/, taking a cue from the spelling, and so they say /ˈwɔːked/, /ˈstɒped/, /ˈmærɪed/ and so on, amongst other possible variations. Work needs to be done here to eliminate the unnecessary vowel sound. Perhaps the most important factor to bear in mind is that such work arises out of the study of a larger grammatical area. As well as the learning of verbs and the formation of past tenses, an essential part of the analysis is the pronunciation difficulties students might have with verb endings. If these are not dealt with, then the language is not being investigated thoroughly.

Consider the lesson plan:

Lesson Plan: Overview			
Teacher: Mark Todd	Level: Intermediate	Date: 11th November	Lesson length: 60min

Main aims of the lesson: To revise some regular simple past tense verbs.

Other aims: To give students listening and speaking practice.

Language to be taught and practised	Work on skills

Structure(s): 🚶 + regular simple past verb.
e.g.: Alice crossed the road, and waited for the minicab.

Which skills will the students practise? (Tick)

Reading	Listening	Speaking	Writing
	✓	✓	

Function:
Narrating.

Specify sub-skills the students will practise (e.g. listening for gist, reading for specific information)

Lexis:
cross, talk, look, call, miss, wait, offer (verbs)
minicab (noun)

Listening for gist.
Listening for specific information.
Story-telling.

Pronunciation:
'-ed' endings are pronounced in a variety of ways: crossed /krɒst/ called /kɔːld/ waited /weɪtɪd/

How will you integrate the skills work and language work?

- Initially presented and practised verbs all appear in the listening activity.
- Students will devise short narratives as an extension of the listening activity.

Potential problems students may have with the language:
Students may use '-ed' as a syllable, so 'crossed' becomes 'cross-ed' /ˈkrɒsed/.

As can be seen from the 'language' section on the left-hand side of the plan, pronunciation here takes its place in the overall analysis of the language being practised in this lesson. The lesson itself is a revision lesson, and so (bearing in mind also the Intermediate level of the students), the grammar, lexis and pronunciation are likely to have been covered before.

Let us look at the actual procedure of the lesson (see facing page).

This is a reasonably standard plan, with the kind of detail expected from teachers undergoing initial or in-service training. Looking through the lesson, we can see that pronunciation is an integral feature. New (or revised) words and verb forms are practised, students listen out for the practised forms in the listening exercises (which also test their understanding of the meaning), and are then given the opportunity to further practise the forms in an extended speaking activity. The teacher also leaves time for correction at the end, where the lesson (including pronunciations of *-ed* endings) can be recapped, and further pronunciation work can be done if necessary.

Aims	Procedure: who does what?
To set context	Teacher (T) shows map of town, and picture of Alice. T tells students (Ss) they will hear story about Alice's evening out. Brainstorm ideas for going out (cinema, club, etc.) Teach 'minicab'.
To elicit/practise vocabulary	T describes the story of Alice's evening. T elicits verbs along the way. T uses pictures, mime as necessary for each verb. T checks concepts as necessary. As verb is elicited, T asks Ss to put it into past tense. T drills past tense of each verb chorally and individually. T drills past tense of each verb in sentences, as in story. T corrects as necessary. NB: Watch pronunciation of '-ed' endings!
Listen for gist	Ss listen to tape x1, and do gist task at same time. (Tape is Alice recounting story, task is to ascertain whether it's the same story we've already been through; also ask if there was a 'happy ending' or not). Ss check answers in pairs. Class feedback.
Listening for specific information	Ss listen to tape for 2nd time, and do specific info. task. (Task is to put pictures in correct order.) Ss check answers in pairs. Class feedback. T plays tape again if necessary. T corrects pronunciation of '-ed' verbs as relevant.
Give further practice of '-ed' verb forms	T gives groups of Ss picture prompts of similar story. Groups devise own version. Form new groups to relate stories. Vote on best one.
Correction phase	Time to recap lesson; do remedial correction and drilling as necessary.

The above Integrated lesson shows pronunciation teaching taking a full role in all stages of a lesson, from planning through to enactment. The next lesson shows how pronunciation work can be slipped into a lesson, when appropriate, in a Remedial or reactive lesson.

Lesson 2: 'Organising a party': Remedial lessons (Pre-Intermediate)
Lesson type: Remedial
Materials: Flashcards of food and drink

The teacher has set up the context of planning a party (for example by showing students a party invitation). She has used picture prompts of food and drink to elicit ideas for things which people might take to the party. She then tells the students that they are invited, and asks a few of them what they might bring along with them, eliciting the sentence *I'll bring x*, where the *x* can be any item of food or drink. The sentence is drilled both chorally and individually, using one of the items of vocabulary (e.g. *I'll bring some pizza*). The teacher then uses her flashcards to elicit the sentence pattern again with other items of vocabulary in turn. Each sentence is again drilled chorally and individually:

I'll bring some pizza. I'll bring some cake.

I'll bring some salad. I'll bring some wine.

As a subsequent practice activity, students have been given the task of planning their own party. This gives them the opportunity to use the sentences which have been practised so far, as well as the chance to add other relevant language (e.g. *I'll bring some CDs*, or *I'll write the invitations*).

In the course of this activity some of the students have had difficulty in pronouncing new items, and so a major role for the teacher is in providing Remedial correction. This is an inevitable and necessary part of the processes of both teaching and learning a language. For example, during the drilling stage, a student mispronounces *wine* as /vaɪn/ (i.e. he repeats the sentence as *I'll bring some* /vaɪn/). The teacher encourages the student to have another go, by saying *I'll bring some...*, leaving the sentence open for completion. It is always a good idea to allow students the opportunity to correct themselves. It may be that the student can pronounce the word correctly, but this is simply a slip of the tongue. Let's imagine that the student again repeats the word as /vaɪn/. The teacher then invites the other students to provide a correction (for example by asking *Can anyone help?*). Not only does this ensure the whole class is involved, but it also helps the teacher to decide if this pronunciation problem is particular to the original student, or if others are having difficulty with it too. If other students cannot provide the correct pronunciation, then the teacher knows that it is necessary to work on that word again at class level, through remedial drilling.

Later on in the 'party' lesson, the drilling stage was followed up by groupwork or pairwork, where students were given the opportunity to further practise the structure and vocabulary. The teacher's main role during such an activity is usually to monitor what is going on, making a note of any difficulties the students might have. These difficulties might be with the structure (e.g. a student might say *I bring...*, or *I bringing...*), with vocabulary (e.g. a student might forget a word, or use the wrong word), or with pronunciation (e.g. *I'll bring some* /vaɪn/, or *I'll* /brɪŋk/ *some wine*).

Intervention at this stage by the teacher is not usually necessary, unless for some reason there is a breakdown in communication. In many instances it is pronunciation which leads to a breakdown, making it necessary for the teacher to intervene in order to get the students back on track. The teacher may, in such instances, need to do some remedial 'on the spot' drilling with a student or a small group of students, so as to make the task achievable once more.

It is always useful to save some time at the end of the lesson in order to both recap what has been covered in a lesson, and to do some Remedial correction. The pronunciation difficulties noted while monitoring earlier on can be dealt with here. This stage can, of course, also cover any other aspects of the lesson which may have given students difficulties.

Progress in language learning tends to be a matter of two steps forward and one step back, and so it is useful to drill again anyway. It is also worth noting that the students' pronunciation during the later activities may not be as accurate as during earlier drilling as they will not have been concentrating so hard on just that aspect of the language.

Generally, Remedial pronunciation work prompted by what has been going on in a class, can be very motivating for students. I can remember the satisfaction of the Japanese learner who finally mastered *I'd like to rent a flat*, and the group of Italian learners who coached each other in saying *He'll have a half pint of Heineken*. Both of these opportunities for working on difficult sounds arose from exchanges in the classroom. Teachers should always be on the lookout for opportunities like these; a student-generated suggestion is more likely to be useful than something provided in good faith by the teacher.

The previous two lessons described the integration of pronunciation work into teaching, the first in a planned way, the second reactively; the next example lesson describes how to base a class period around particular aspects of pronunciation.

The next description shows how a teacher made a specific pronunciation issue the main focus of the class period, thus creating a Practice lesson.

Lesson 3: Minimal pairs: A Practice lesson (Elementary+)

Lesson type: Practice
Materials: Taped listening (optional)

The teacher has noticed that the sounds /æ/ and /ʌ/ cause difficulty for many of the students in his class. They appear to have difficulty in hearing a difference between the two sounds, and also seem to produce neither sound accurately, tending instead to produce a sound which seems to be halfway between the two. The teacher decides therefore to work on these two sounds in a practice activity.

The teacher uses flashcards or draws pictures on the board, to elicit one or two minimal pairs (for example *cat, cut, hat, hut*). These pairs are drilled chorally and individually, to give students plenty of opportunity to listen out for differences, and practise saying them. The teacher then writes the two phonemes on the board, and drills the sounds. He then holds up his pictures, or points to his drawings, asking the students to give the sound for each one.

Students are then given a list of five to ten minimal pairs, which form the basis of the subsequent activity. The teacher asks the students to look through the pairs, and try saying each word to themselves, predicting which sound the words will have. The teacher can then either use a tape recording, or simply say sentences like *It's quite a big cat, Whose is that hut?* etc. For each sentence, the students have to circle the word in their list that they have heard in the sentence. The sentences can be repeated twice, to give the students an opportunity to consider their answers. Students then compare their answers with their neighbours, before feedback is conducted at the class level. The sentences can be repeated again at this stage, if necessary for clarification.

Conclusions

In this chapter we have:
- considered the reasons for teaching pronunciation, with regard to the errors that learners can make and the impact of these errors on successful communication.
- looked at the fact that pronunciation tends to be neglected in classes, and that when it is addressed this is often only done in reaction to specific problems that occur in class.
- asserted that pronunciation needs to be treated as an integral part of language analysis and lesson planning.
- described three kinds of pronunciation lesson: Integrated, Remedial and Practice lessons.
- considered the issue of pronunciation models for students, and suggested that teachers should give models that are natural to them but should also make their students aware of a range of language varieties.
- described various techniques and activities that can be used in class to foster productive and receptive pronunciation skills.
- exemplified these techniques and activities in use in the three different types of pronunciation lesson, showing in the first lesson example how pronunciation issues can be planned into a lesson.

Looking ahead

Having looked at Integrated, Remedial and Practice lesson types, and how pronunciation can be worked on in the classroom, we will now start to consider the various features of pronunciation in more depth. The next two chapters investigate the nature of the English vowel and consonant sounds. We will also look at how they can be taught in an Integrated way, Practised and worked on Remedially.

3 Vowels

- The characteristics of the 'pure' vowel sounds
- The characteristics of diphthongs
- Raising awareness of vowel sounds
- Sample lessons
    - Lesson 1: 'Phonemic bingo': Particular vowel sounds
    - Lesson 2: 'Noughts and crosses': Particular vowel sounds
    - Lesson 3: 'Snap': Particular vowel sounds
    - Lesson 4: 'Stand up and be counted': Vowel sounds/schwa /ə/
    - Lesson 5: 'Which vowel am I?': Vowel sounds
    - Lesson 6: Collaborative writing: Vowel sounds
- Further ideas for activities

The characteristics of the 'pure' vowel sounds

We saw in Chapter 1 that vowels are articulated when a voiced airstream is shaped using the tongue and the lips to modify the overall shape of the mouth. English speakers generally use twelve pure vowels and eight diphthongs.

If you try saying /iː/ /e/ /æ/ /ɒ/ /ɔː/ /uː/ out loud, you should be able to feel that your tongue changes position in your mouth, yet it doesn't actually obstruct the airflow. Try moving smoothly from one sound to the next, without stopping. You will also be aware of the shape of your lips changing, and your lower jaw moving. It is these basic movements which give vowels their chief characteristics.

It is important to keep in mind what it is exactly which makes a phoneme valid as a unit for analysis; the distinctions between phonemes hold, in that they are units which differentiate between word meanings. In the previous chapter we looked at minimal pairs, such as *soap* /səʊp/ and *soup* /suːp/ to illustrate this principle.

It is useful to mention here too one of the principles behind phonemic analysis: it was mentioned in Chapter 1 that we may pronounce particular sounds in different ways. Your pronunciation of /r/ may be slightly different to mine, yet we manage to understand each other. These two different pronunciations of /r/ are known as **allophones**. (Allophones are usually indicated by being enclosed in square brackets.) Though there may be subtle differences in articulation, they do not lead to a change of meaning. In phonemic transcription, each symbol is therefore used as a representation of the 'principal' sound of a 'family' of similar sounds. Such subtle differences are not important for the classroom, and so we will concentrate on general descriptions for vowel sounds.

The pure vowel sounds

The word 'pure' here is used to differentiate single vowel sounds from diphthongs, which we will consider later. The sounds have been divided up into categories, according to the characteristics of their articulation, and each category begins with a brief outline. All of the sounds, together with the example words, are on the CD.

The tables on the following pages give the following information. A diagram of the 'vowel space' (or the part of the mouth and throat which is used in the production of vowels) is shown. The dot on each diagram represents the height of the tongue, and also the part of the tongue which is raised. The phonemic symbol is shown. The characteristics of the sound are described. Tongue and lip positions are referred to. Example words are given, to illustrate the spelling/sound relationships.

Reference is also made to lip positions; the illustrations below show the basic lip positions which are used in describing the articulation of vowel sounds. We notice, of course, constant movement in real speech, as we move from sound to sound and switch between vowels and consonants. However, if we take a 'snapshot' view of lip positions, this is what we see:

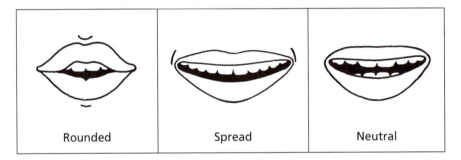

| Rounded | Spread | Neutral |

Rounded: the lips are pushed forward into the shape of a circle. Example sound: /ʊ/

Spread: the corners of the lips are moved away from each other, as when smiling. Example sound: /iː/

Neutral: the lips are not noticeably rounded or spread. Example sound: /ə/

The languages referred to in the following diagrams are as follows:

Arabic (A)	Chinese (C)	French (F)	German (G)
Greek (Gk)	Indian languages (Ind)	Italian (It)	Japanese (J)
Portuguese (P)	Russian (R)	Scandinavian languages (Sc)	Spanish (Sp)
Turkish (Tu)			

Close vowels

For close vowels the tongue is quite high in the mouth. Moving from /iː/ through to /uː/, we also notice the different positions of the tongue; /iː/ is a front vowel, and /uː/ is a back vowel.

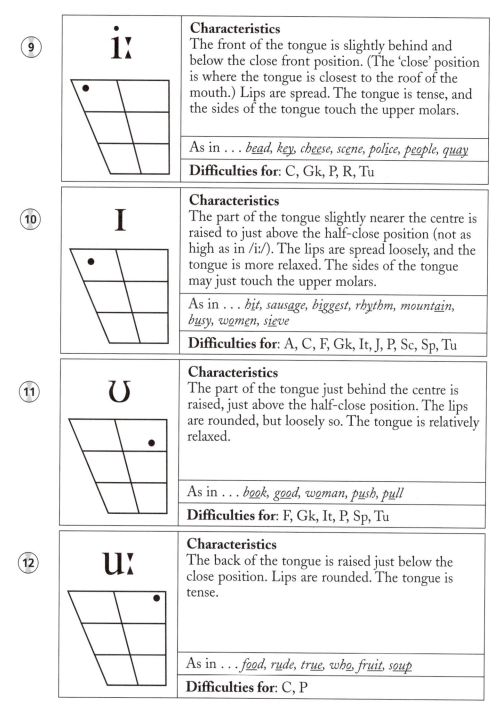

(9) iː	**Characteristics** The front of the tongue is slightly behind and below the close front position. (The 'close' position is where the tongue is closest to the roof of the mouth.) Lips are spread. The tongue is tense, and the sides of the tongue touch the upper molars.
	As in . . . _bead_, _key_, _cheese_, _scene_, _police_, _people_, _quay_
	Difficulties for: C, Gk, P, R, Tu
(10) I	**Characteristics** The part of the tongue slightly nearer the centre is raised to just above the half-close position (not as high as in /iː/). The lips are spread loosely, and the tongue is more relaxed. The sides of the tongue may just touch the upper molars.
	As in . . . _hit_, _sausage_, _biggest_, _rhythm_, _mountain_, _busy_, _women_, _sieve_
	Difficulties for: A, C, F, Gk, It, J, P, Sc, Sp, Tu
(11) ʊ	**Characteristics** The part of the tongue just behind the centre is raised, just above the half-close position. The lips are rounded, but loosely so. The tongue is relatively relaxed.
	As in . . . _book_, _good_, _woman_, _push_, _pull_
	Difficulties for: F, Gk, It, P, Sp, Tu
(12) uː	**Characteristics** The back of the tongue is raised just below the close position. Lips are rounded. The tongue is tense.
	As in . . . _food_, _rude_, _true_, _who_, _fruit_, _soup_
	Difficulties for: C, P

Mid vowels

For mid vowels the tongue is neither high nor low in the mouth. Moving from /e/ through to /ɔː/, we also notice the different positions of the tongue; /e/ is a front vowel, and /ɔː/ is a back vowel.

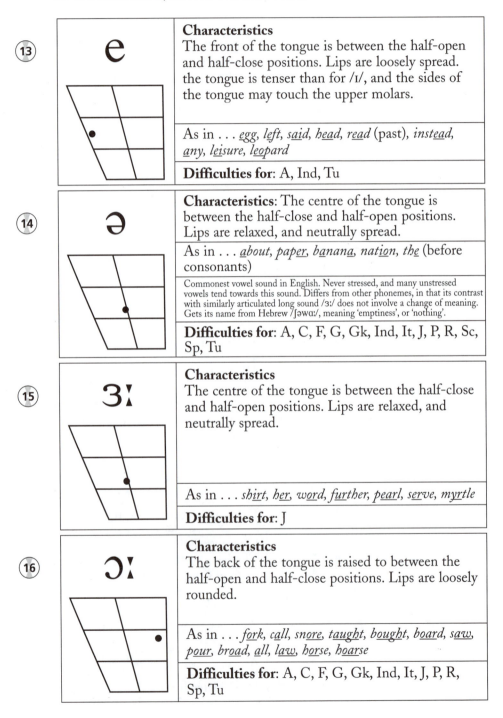

13	e	**Characteristics** The front of the tongue is between the half-open and half-close positions. Lips are loosely spread. the tongue is tenser than for /ɪ/, and the sides of the tongue may touch the upper molars.
		As in . . . *egg, left, said, head, read* (past), *instead, any, leisure, leopard*
		Difficulties for: A, Ind, Tu
14	ə	**Characteristics**: The centre of the tongue is between the half-close and half-open positions. Lips are relaxed, and neutrally spread.
		As in . . . *about, paper, banana, nation, the* (before consonants)
		Commonest vowel sound in English. Never stressed, and many unstressed vowels tend towards this sound. Differs from other phonemes, in that its contrast with similarly articulated long sound /ɜː/ does not involve a change of meaning. Gets its name from Hebrew /ʃəwɑː/, meaning 'emptiness', or 'nothing'.
		Difficulties for: A, C, F, G, Gk, Ind, It, J, P, R, Sc, Sp, Tu
15	3ː	**Characteristics** The centre of the tongue is between the half-close and half-open positions. Lips are relaxed, and neutrally spread.
		As in . . . *shirt, her, word, further, pearl, serve, myrtle*
		Difficulties for: J
16	ɔː	**Characteristics** The back of the tongue is raised to between the half-open and half-close positions. Lips are loosely rounded.
		As in . . . *fork, call, snore, taught, bought, board, saw, pour, broad, all, law, horse, hoarse*
		Difficulties for: A, C, F, G, Gk, Ind, It, J, P, R, Sp, Tu

Open vowels

For open vowels, the tongue is low in the mouth. Moving from /æ/ through to /ɒ/, we also notice the different positions of the tongue; /æ/ is a front vowel, and /ɒ/ is a back vowel.

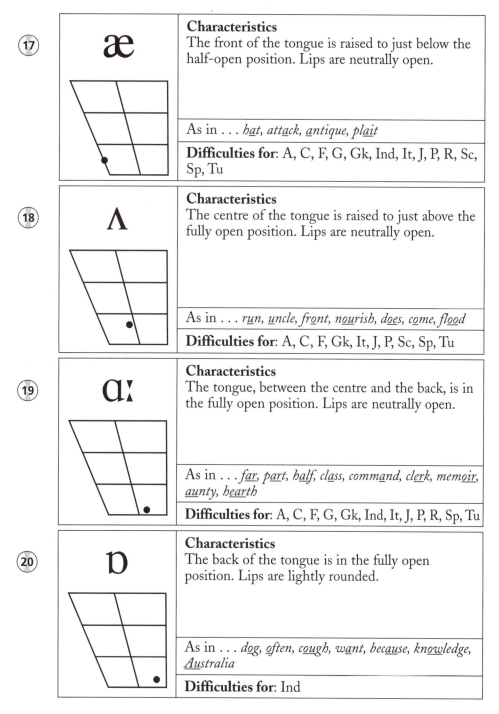

17

æ

Characteristics
The front of the tongue is raised to just below the half-open position. Lips are neutrally open.

As in . . . h*a*t, att*a*ck, *a*ntique, pl*ai*t

Difficulties for: A, C, F, G, Gk, Ind, It, J, P, R, Sc, Sp, Tu

18

ʌ

Characteristics
The centre of the tongue is raised to just above the fully open position. Lips are neutrally open.

As in . . . r*u*n, *u*ncle, fr*o*nt, n*ou*rish, d*oe*s, c*o*me, fl*oo*d

Difficulties for: A, C, F, Gk, It, J, P, Sc, Sp, Tu

19

ɑː

Characteristics
The tongue, between the centre and the back, is in the fully open position. Lips are neutrally open.

As in . . . f*a*r, p*a*rt, h*a*lf, cl*a*ss, comm*a*nd, cl*e*rk, mem*oi*r, *au*nty, h*ea*rth

Difficulties for: A, C, F, G, Gk, Ind, It, J, P, R, Sp, Tu

20

ɒ

Characteristics
The back of the tongue is in the fully open position. Lips are lightly rounded.

As in . . . d*o*g, *o*ften, c*ou*gh, w*a*nt, bec*au*se, kn*ow*ledge, *A*ustralia

Difficulties for: Ind

33

Difficulties in analysing vowel sounds

Aside from the articulatory differences, the length of short and long vowels (the long vowel phonemes being followed by the lengthening symbol /ː/), is best seen as relative. For example, consider the sound /ɪ/ in the words *bid* /bɪd/ and *bit* /bɪt/. If you say the two words over to yourself a few times it becomes apparent that the /ɪ/ in *bid* is longer than the /ɪ/ in *bit*. The same phenomenon is noticed in the minimal pair *badge* /bædʒ/ and *batch* /bætʃ/. Essentially, the rule in operation here is that a short vowel is longer before a voiced consonant. Taking the investigation further would reveal that they are actually more likely to be longer before certain types of voiced consonant too. Interestingly this is not true of all languages, yet it is a distinctive feature of English. There are further aspects of vowel length which we will explore in Chapter 5. You should keep in mind the premise that each symbol represents a 'family' of sounds.

The characteristics of diphthongs

A crude definition of a diphthong might be 'a combination of vowel sounds'. A slightly closer analysis shows us that there is a **glide** (or movement of the tongue, lips and jaw) from one pure vowel sound to another. The first sound in each phoneme is longer and louder than the second in English, but not in all languages. If we listen to the word *house* (the diphthong in question is /aʊ/), we can hear that the /a/ part of the sound is longer than the final /ʊ/ part. If you try making the /ʊ/ part longer, you will hear the difference.

English is usually described as having eight diphthongs, and they can be usefully grouped in the following way:

Centring diphthongs end with a glide towards /ə/. They are called 'centring' because /ə/ is a central vowel (refer to the /ə/ table on page 32).

Examples:
1 *clearing* /ɪə/
2 *sure* /ʊə/
3 *there* /eə/

Closing diphthongs end with a glide towards /ɪ/ or towards /ʊ/. The glide is towards a higher position in the mouth.

Examples:
4 *they* /eɪ/
5 *boy* /ɔɪ/
6 *mighty* /aɪ/
7 *go* /əʊ/
8 *now* /aʊ/

The following tables show the characteristics of the eight diphthong sounds, in the same manner as the previous vowel tables. Bear in mind that while we have mentioned a combination of sounds, or more accurately a glide from one tongue position to another, diphthongs are perceived as one sound, and should be treated as such. The glide in each diagram is shown as an arrow from the tongue position of the initial sound (represented by a dot) to the finishing position of the second element of the diphthong.

Centring diphthongs

(21)

Iə

Characteristics
The glide begins in the position for /ɪ/, moving down and back towards /ə/. The lips are neutral, but with a small movement from spread to open.

As in . . . _beer_, _beard_, _fear_, _pierce_, _Ian_, _here_, _idea_

Difficulties for: A, C, F, G, Gk, Ind, It, J, P, R, Sc, Sp, Tu

(22)

ʊə

Characteristics
The glide begins in the position for /ʊ/, moving forwards and down towards /ə/. The lips are loosely rounded, becoming neutrally spread.

As in . . . *_sure_, _moor_, _tour_, _obscure_

*Quite a rare diphthong. Many speakers replace it with /ɔː/

Difficulties for: A, C, F, G, Gk, Ind, It, J, P, R, Sc, Sp, Tu

(23)

eə

Characteristics
The glide begins in the position for /e/, moving back towards /ə/. The lips remain neutrally open.

As in . . . _where_, _wear_, _chair_, _dare_, _stare_, _there_

Difficulties for: A, C, F, G, Gk, Ind, It, J, P, R, Sc, Sp, Tu

Closing diphthongs ending in /ɪ/

(24)

eɪ

Characteristics
The glide begins in the position for /e/, moving up and slightly back towards /ɪ/. The lips are spread.

As in . . . _cake_, _way_, _weigh_, _say_, _pain_, _they_, _vein_

Difficulties for: A, C, F, G, Ind, It, Sc, Sp, Tu

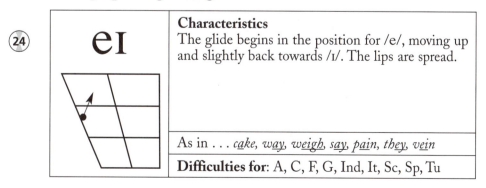

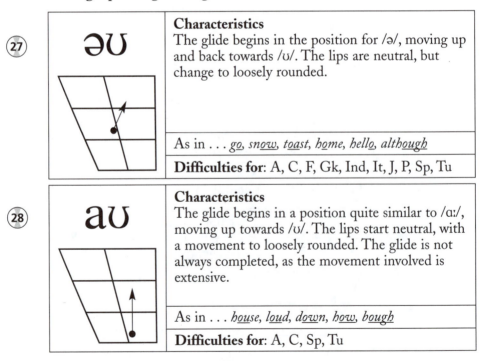

25

ɔɪ

Characteristics

The glide begins in the position for /ɔː/, moving up and forward towards /ɪ/. The lips start open and rounded, and change to neutral.

As in . . . _toy_, _avoid_, _voice_, _enjoy_, _boy_

Difficulties for: A, C, Ind, Sp, Tu

26

aɪ

Characteristics

The glide begins in an open position, between front and centre, moving up and slightly forward towards /ɪ/. The lips move from neutral, to loosely spread.

As in . . . _high_, _tie_, _buy_, _kite_, _might_, _cry_, _eye_

Difficulties for: A, C, Sp, Tu

Closing diphthongs ending in /ʊ/

27

əʊ

Characteristics

The glide begins in the position for /ə/, moving up and back towards /ʊ/. The lips are neutral, but change to loosely rounded.

As in . . . _go_, _snow_, _toast_, _home_, _hello_, _although_

Difficulties for: A, C, F, Gk, Ind, It, J, P, Sp, Tu

28

aʊ

Characteristics

The glide begins in a position quite similar to /ɑː/, moving up towards /ʊ/. The lips start neutral, with a movement to loosely rounded. The glide is not always completed, as the movement involved is extensive.

As in . . . _house_, _loud_, _down_, _how_, _bough_

Difficulties for: A, C, Sp, Tu

Raising awareness of vowel sounds

The aim of dealing with a sound in isolation in the classroom should be to help learners towards more successful pronunciation of the particular phoneme which is having an effect on communication and intelligibility. In a class which is learning general English, it would not make sense to divert attention away from that purpose in order to teach the complete catalogue of English phonemes, unless the teacher and the class have decided that it would be advantageous.

Sounds should be dealt with in class as and when the need arises. This can be done remedially as a reaction to a communicative difficulty which occurs in class, or because the sounds are an important feature of the grammar or lexis being taught. Sounds can also be practised in their own right, as a way of focusing on a particular area of difficulty.

In spoken language all sounds are, of course, important, but at times certain sounds seem central to the success or otherwise of communication. While L1 English speakers seem able to tolerate a lot of variation in vowel sounds (for example the North/South differences in British English, such as *bath*, pronounced as /bæθ/ or /bɑːθ/), poor pronunciation can affect intelligibility. Native speakers do accept without too much difficulty some variety in vowel sounds, and certainly the trained ear of a teacher can cope with a wide range of variation, yet vowels present learners with particular difficulties. Accuracy often involves losing a vowel sound from an utterance (seen with /e/ in the 'Alice' lesson plan in Chapter 2) as much as using the correct sound (seen with the *soap* /səʊp/ and *soup* /suːp/, and *paper* /ˈpeɪpə/ and *pepper* /ˈpepə/ minimal pairs also mentioned in Chapter 2).

Every time someone speaks in class, pronunciation is a matter for consideration. The following suggestions can be used to raise general awareness of vowel sounds. The suggestions are followed by some sample lessons, and other activities.

Using a phonemic chart

This is certainly to be encouraged, especially if the chart is laid out so as to explain the relationships between sounds in a 'student friendly' way. Students will need some initial coaching through the chart, but using one can help enhance independent learning outside the classroom. The learners' reference chart of English sounds is on page 143. The chart aims to give the information that students need in order to be able to use it independently. Have one in your class, give students their own copy, and encourage them to refer to it when they need to. Use it periodically in conjunction with dictionary study, and use it both for teaching 'new' sounds and the correction of sounds already covered.

Drilling, repetition and associating sounds with ideas

Drilling was discussed at length in Chapter 2, and for vowel sounds it remains one of the teacher's best tools. Sounds can be drilled along with the structures or lexis being practised, in order to show how they 'fit in' to the general environment of the language being worked on in class.

If a particular focus is needed, sounds can be worked on singly. Here are some (occasionally light-hearted) suggestions to help make the vowel sounds more memorable for students. The teacher can model, and students can copy the sound. The suggestions are intended to help students associate sounds with particular ideas, which, for most learners, will make them easier to remember.

Sound	Suggestion
Vowels	
iː	A 'smiling' sound. Smile widely, make and hold the sound. Demonstrate that it is a 'long' sound.
ɪ	Make the sound, and make it obviously short. If necessary, contrast it with /iː/.
ʊ	A short sound. Exaggerate the forward position of your lips. One way into this sound is to ask students what noise a gorilla makes!
uː	Make and hold the sound. Use a 'rising then falling' intonation, as if you've heard something surprising, or some interesting gossip (uuUUuu). Demonstrate that it is a 'long' sound.
e	A short sound. Make the sound, and point out the loosely spread position of your lips.
ə	The 'Friday afternoon' sound. Relax your whole body, slump your shoulders, relax your face and mouth, and say /ə/, as though completely exhausted.
ɜː	The 'something horrible' sound. Make and hold the sound, curl your upper lip, and pretend to look at something nasty. Look in the litter bin, if there is one to hand. Demonstrate that it is a 'long' sound.
ɔː	The 'either/or' sound. Liken it to the word *or*. Demonstrate that it is a 'long' sound.
æ	Make the sound, and point out the neutrally open shape of your lips.
ʌ	Make the sound, and throw your head back slightly as you do it. This works well if contrasted with /æ/.
ɑː	The 'holding the baby' sound. Place your arms as though holding a baby, and say /ɑː/. Demonstrate that it is a 'long' sound.
ɒ	Make the sound, and point out your lightly rounded lips.

Diphthongs	For all diphthongs, one of the best techniques is to get students to make and hold the first element, then slowly move to the second. Finish off by making the sound at a 'normal' speed. Some other suggestions are made below.
ɪə	Make the sound while tugging your ear.
ʊə	Hold the first sound, and move to the second.
eə	Liken this to the word *air*. Point to your hair. Say *over there*, or *on the chair*. All will give good examples of the sound, which you can then isolate.
eɪ	Pretend not to hear someone, and say *eh?*.
ɔɪ	Words work best here: *toy, boy, enjoy.*
aɪ	Make the sound and point to your eye.
əʊ	*Oh, hello*, said slowly, and exaggerated a little, works well.
aʊ	The 'shut your finger in the door' sound. Pretending to do this and making the sound while pulling a 'pained' expression works rather well!

You may or may not feel comfortable using some of these suggestions with your class; if in doubt, the best advice is not to do it, but devise your own alternative to suit your classroom manner and style. These are all only suggestions.

It can help also to associate sounds with pictures that illustrate the sound (for example a picture of a sheep with /iː/, a picture of a hat with /æ/, and so on). Some students find this a good aid to memory. But if the picture illustrates a word which the student knows, and is in the habit of mispronouncing, this can simply lead to the vowel difficulty becoming further entrenched.

The sounds need obviously to be associated with the phonemic symbols; you need not worry about whether or not students can 'cope' with being introduced to phonemic script, as long as you are clear about explaining the purpose of it. Show students the symbols being used in dictionaries, and aim to use them regularly, clearly and consistently. Care needs to be taken, however, if students are not familiar with roman script (for example beginner Chinese or Arabic students, or those more used to Cyrillic script), to differentiate between phonemic symbols and the letters we use for writing. You can, for example, use a different coloured pen on the board for phonemic script, or save one section of the board for it; however you do it, be consistent, so as to minimise any potential problems. I have used phonemic script successfully with students ranging from complete beginners to very advanced; if you treat its use as a normal part of your teaching, and not as something 'special', or 'technical', you will have a very valuable classroom tool at your disposal.

'Halfway house' sounds

If students are having problems producing a particular sound, you can treat the sound that they are having difficulty with as a 'halfway house' between two others, as shown in the following chart. Students should start by making and holding the 'home' sound, and without stopping, they should make the necessary gradual adjustments of articulation as they head for their 'destination'. Students don't actually have to reach the destination sound, but en route, they will find the sound they are aiming for.

'Home' sound	'Halfway house'	'Destination'
iː	ɪ	e
ɪ	e	æ
e	æ	ɑː
æ	ʌ	ɒ
æ	ɑː	ɒ
ɑː	ɒ	ɔː
ɒ	ɔː	ʊ
ɔː	ʊ	uː
e	ə or ɜː	ɔː

The exact 'halfway house' sound you are trying to get students to produce will not necessarily be accurately made in all cases, but doing this procedure can at least get students nearer to producing the sound in question. The teacher needs to exercise judgement in order to let students know when the 'halfway house' has been reached. The idea can also help students to appreciate the subtle differences between vowels, and also, in some cases, show how English sounds differ from similar sounds in L1.

Sample lessons

The activities in the following sample lessons can be used in various ways, whether for raising awareness of a pronunciation issue or as revision of something already covered. However, they are all Practice lessons (see page 14) and thus can form the basis for an extended lesson on pronunciation. Some of the activities can be used for practising consonants, and some necessarily include study and practice of both vowels and consonants. This reflects the nature of what goes on in the classroom; teachers will have to, eventually, deal with vowels and consonants together.

Lesson 1: 'Phonemic bingo': Particular vowel sounds (All levels)

Lesson type: Practice
Materials: Bingo cards

Make some bingo cards with a good range of phonemic vowel symbols on each. Each one should have the same number of sounds on it. Make sure that you have enough to go round. In monolingual classes, the sounds used can reflect typical problem sounds for speakers of the students' L1. In multilingual classes, the sounds can reflect the range of difficulties for the students present.

Example cards are shown below:

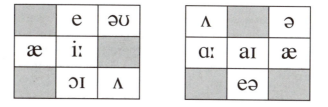

To play the game, students are given a card each. The sounds are called out one by one, and students cross off or cover up the ones they have on their cards. The way of 'calling' the sounds can be varied according to the needs and abilities of the class.

One variation involves calling out words instead of sounds; students then have to work out whether or not the words contain vowels which match any on their cards. Teachers could also ask students to write another example word on their card as they cross sounds off. The 'caller' would have to allow time for this of course! When a student has filled up her card, she shouts 'Bingo', and the card is checked.

A part of the learning value of an activity like this comes in going through the winning card with the whole class, to see if the student who has crossed all the sounds off first has got them right. The activity can equally well be used for practising consonant sounds.

Lesson 2: 'Noughts and crosses': Particular vowel sounds (All levels)

Lesson type: Practice
Materials: Noughts and crosses grids, with vowel phonemes written on.

ɪ	ʌ	e
ə	ɒ	æ
ɔː	iː	ɑː

A grid with nine 'squares' is used, each square having a vowel phoneme. The phonemes used should reflect the sounds which cause particular difficulty for the students in the class. Students should work in pairs, with one copy of the grid for each pair. The first student chooses a square, and provides a word which contains that sound. If they get it right, they put a 'nought' in the square. Then it is the second student's turn; if their suggestion is correct for their nominated square, they put a cross. (You can use different coloured counters, or different denominations of coins, if you want to hang onto the grids for later use.) If a student gets a word wrong (i.e. it does not contain the sound for the square they are trying to win), the second student can try to win the square.

The winner is the first to complete a straight line of three. Although noughts and crosses seems almost universal, the activity has a different slant here, and so the teacher should demonstrate the activity to the whole class, just to make sure that students know what to do. Students can then play the game in pairs. It can also be played in teams, in which case the teams need to be given time to confer. It also helps if a spokesperson is nominated for each team. To provide more focus prior to the game, give students/teams time to look at the 'grid' and think up words in advance, without the use of a dictionary. The activity can equally well be used for practising consonant sounds.

Lesson 3: 'Snap': Particular vowel sounds (All levels)

Lesson type: Practice
Materials: Sets of cards with vowel sounds written on

The teacher needs to prepare several class sets of cards with a single vowel sound on each card. It is recommended that each set has an even number of each vowel phoneme. A lot of preparation is therefore required, but if suitably sturdy materials are used (e.g. card, written on then laminated) the sets can be used many times over. The game is played just like the card game 'Snap', in that cards are dealt out, and two to five players take it in turns to lay them down; the first to shout 'snap' when a matching pair are consecutively laid down wins all the cards that are on the table. To make it more than just a visual game, the instruction can be given that instead of shouting 'snap' when a pair occurs, the players have to shout out a word containing the sound. If the word is not correct, the other player(s) can have a go at providing a word. The teacher can act as referee if necessary.

Alternatively, known or recently studied words can be used on the cards, but make sure you don't put the same word twice and try to ensure a high number of words which share at least one vowel phoneme. It helps to underline the letter(s) corresponding to vowel sounds. When two words are laid down consecutively which share a vowel sound, the players shout 'snap', and the first to do so wins that 'hand'.

Another variation is to make two sets of cards: one with vowel symbols, and the other with recently studied or known words (or some new ones too, if you want to encourage prediction skills). Players take turns to turn over one card at a time from either pile. Whenever the sound on the top vowel card is found in the word on top of the other pile, players again compete to shout 'snap'. Whichever version of the game is used, it is useful to demonstrate it to the class first, to make sure students are familiar with the rules.

Lesson 4: 'Stand up and be counted': Vowel sounds/schwa (All levels)

Lesson type: Practice
Materials: Cards with vowel sounds on

This task is useful for vowel recognition, and uses the students' own suggestions for words. The teacher asks students to write down three or four words each. These can be recently studied words, words from that day's lesson, or simply random ones. Give each student a card with a vowel phoneme on. Make sure that /ə/ is included. Each student reads out their words in turn, and all the students listen out for which vowel sounds appear in the word. If the sound they have on their card appears in the word that has been read out, they stand up. The student who has the /ə/ card should, by the end of the activity, have been required to stand up more often than others. This activity is very useful for showing the high incidence of /ə/. This is usually demonstrated by this activity, but not always!

Lesson 5: 'Which vowel am I?': Vowel sounds (All levels)

Lesson type: Practice
Materials: Sticky labels with vowel sounds on

The teacher places a sticky label with a vowel phoneme on each student's back. Students move around the classroom, looking at the notes on each other's backs, and tell each other words which include that sound. When they have worked out what their sound is, students have to write their name on the board, and write up the phonemic symbol also. The task can take the form of a race to be first, a race not to be last, or simply a task to be achieved without the competitive element, if you prefer.

To make it more difficult, depending on the level of the class, the teacher can instruct students that the words they say must not start with the sound, but must include it. Also the teacher should tell students that they mustn't cheat, by deliberately giving wrong words! To help prevent this, and also to encourage a co-operative atmosphere, the students can be divided into two teams. The team members help each other guess their sounds, and the first team to get all of them correct, wins.

A slightly easier variation is to have a list of words on the board, each of which includes an example of one of the phonemes assigned to students. Students then have to write their name on the board next to the word which matches 'their' sound, when they have worked it out. Of course, the students need to be told that they must not say any of the words that appear on the board.

Lesson 6: Collaborative writing: Vowel sounds (Elementary+)

Lesson type: Practice
Materials: Strips of paper for writing on

Studying vowel sounds gives plenty of scope for working with rhyme. Collaborative poem writing can be a rewarding group- or pair-based activity. The teacher chooses a current problem sound. In this example the sound is /iː/. Students are asked to write lines of a poem, according to the following criteria: Some lines should start with a subject pronoun (*I, you, he, she, it*, etc.), and they should only use the past simple. (You can, of course, use other criteria; these simply ensure a degree of readability.) The last word in each line should end with the sound being worked on. The lines are written on strips of paper, which can be collected in a box, or put in a pile.

The following are random lines produced by an Intermediate class who did this activity (although admittedly, not all the sentences here use the past simple):

Is this seat free?
He had a cup of tea
I damaged my knee
Would you like coffee?
'To be' or not 'to be'
I sat under a tree
I got stung by a bee
Yesterday I lost my key
I want to be free

Groups then select a given number of lines from the box or pile, and organise them into 'poems', to be read out later to the class. The lines above were reorganised into the following masterpiece:

Yesterday I lost my key
I sat under a tree
I damaged my knee
I got stung by a bee
He had a cup of tea
Would you like coffee?
I want to be free
'To be' or not 'to be'

The finished piece may not be great poetry, but the task focuses students successfully on the sound in question. Students might also be given the chance to make their poem read better (e.g. *Yesterday I lost my key, So I sat under a tree...*). Also, it is noticeable that most of the lines above end in the easiest choice for /iː/, the *-ee* spelling. Alternative spellings for /iː/ can then be looked at in detail at the beginning, middle and ends of words (e.g. *e-mail, easy, Israeli*).

Further ideas for activities

'Phonemic crosswords'
The teacher needs to prepare a basic crossword grid. It's a good idea to spend some time producing a few blank versions, which you can photocopy (or print out if your computer skills are up to it) and adapt to suit the needs of your class. Clues can be in alphabetic script and the answers in phonemic script, or clues phonemic and answers alphabetic, or both clues and answers in phonemic script. (A phonemic crossword clearly requires knowledge of both vowel and consonant phonemes.) Bear in mind how familiar and confident your students are with the phonemes, and aim to make the task achievable, and include a combination of known and recently studied words among your answers. It can help to keep clues related to a particular subject area. To focus clearly on vowel sounds, make sure at least some words 'cross' each other on these sounds. The small example here gives both clues and answers:

¹ɒ	k	²t	ə	p	ə	³s
s		ɔː				iː
⁴t	ɜː	t	ə	l		l
r		ə			⁵ɒ	
⁶ɪ	n	s	e	k	t	s
tʃ					ə	

Across
1 Sea animal with eight legs.
4 Swimming version of 2 down.
6 These animals all have six legs.

Down
1 Big bird which can't fly.
2 Very slow animal, with four legs and a shell.
3 Animal that lives in the sea and on land, and has flippers.
5 These brown mammals live in rivers or the sea and eat fish.

'Irritable vowels'

This is not so much an activity, as a reminder to both teacher and students to pay attention to vowel sounds which have been causing difficulty. It's a good idea to get into the habit of setting aside some time to work on difficult sounds, for example during the last lesson of the week, and to set some homework based on those sounds. Homework activities connected with pronunciation of vowels could include exercises on paper (like matching exercises, crosswords, finding words with particular sounds in a text, etc.) or could be based on awareness of sounds in everyday conversation. For example, students might be asked to consider situations they have been in, or conversations they have had, in which particular sounds have caused difficulties. These could be productive difficulties (i.e. somebody else had difficulty understanding the student), or receptive (the student had difficulty understanding something within a conversation). Students need not be tied down to conversations, either; a lot of very useful work can come from listening to the radio, or watching television and videos. Videos are particularly useful, as students can rewind the bits they have had difficulty understanding, and try again. Particular sounds which have caused difficulty can then be noted down and brought up in class for further study.

Students can be asked to nominate which sound has caused them the most difficulty that week. Each student can be asked in turn, or students can share their thoughts in small groups, asking the teacher for help with sounds as necessary. Students can be asked also for a word which includes that sound. They could also be asked to give suggestions for words for other students to note down. This has the added advantage of helping everyone in the class to concentrate on the sounds and improving classroom communication by helping to familiarise students with each other's difficulties.

Students might be asked to act as monitors for each other for a lesson, a day or a whole week. At the beginning students might say 'I'd like you to listen out for my pronunciation of /æ/'. This works best if students only ask their neighbours in the class; otherwise there is too much for everyone to listen out for. However, narrowing down the task of mastering vowel sounds can pay enormous dividends for individual students, and keeps an achievable aim in mind. Regular use of such ideas in the class also encourages students to keep pronunciation in mind while concentrating on activities which are primarily concerned with grammar and vocabulary.

'Vowels-U-Like'
As a flipside of the 'irritable vowels' idea, students can also be given time to either congratulate themselves on mastering a particular vowel sound, or have time to practise something they are comfortable with. Students can also be encouraged to point out how well their classmates have progressed with sounds. While we have said that it isn't worth focusing on sounds if they aren't causing difficulties, it's also important to sometimes let students use what they already have, or use what they have recently mastered, without being set too much of a challenge.

Teachers should aim to involve students in setting the agenda for classroom pronunciation work, through helping them to be conscious of the particular sounds which they have difficulty in either recognising or producing.

Conclusions

In this chapter we have:
- considered the characteristics of the 'pure' vowel sounds and diphthongs and seen that vowel sounds can be described in terms of tongue and lip positions. Diphthongs, on the other hand, can be described in terms of a movement (or 'glide') from one vowel position to another.
- studied tables showing the characteristics of the vowel sounds including the tongue and lip positions for each, their phonemic symbols, example words, and we have listed the first languages of those speakers who may have productive difficulties with these sounds in English.
- considered ways of raising awareness of vowel sounds in the classroom.
- considered reasons for using a phonemic chart to promote learner independence.
- considered a variety of classroom activities for focusing on vowel sounds in the classroom.
- suggested that teachers should involve their students in deciding on priorities for classroom pronunciation work, through helping them to be aware of their pronunciation difficulties.

Looking ahead

In Chapter 4 we will:
- look closely at consonant sounds, describing how they are articulated and which speakers might have difficulties in producing which particular sounds.
- look at ways of raising awareness of consonant sounds.
- look at activities which can be used in class to focus on consonant sounds.

4 Consonants

- **The characteristics of the consonant sounds**
- **Raising awareness of consonant sounds**
- **Sample lessons**
  - **Lesson 1: 'Hangman': Consonant and vowel sounds**
  - **Lesson 2: 'I'm going to the party': Particular consonant sounds**
  - **Lesson 3: Phonemic word search: Consonant and vowel sounds**
  - **Lesson 4: Advertising slogans: Particular consonant sounds**
  - **Lesson 5: Running dictation: Particular consonant/vowel sounds**
- **Further ideas for activities**

The characteristics of the consonant sounds

As we saw in Chapter 1, consonants are formed by interrupting, restricting or diverting the airflow in a variety of ways. There are three ways of describing the consonant sounds:

1. the manner of articulation
2. the place of articulation
3. the force of articulation

The **manner of articulation** refers to the interaction between the various articulators and the airstream. For example, with plosive sounds, the articulators act in such a way that the air is temporarily trapped, and then suddenly released. The manners of articulation are:

plosive	affricate	fricative
nasal	lateral	approximant

These are the categories used for classification in the tables in this chapter. For more details on these terms, see page 6.

Describing the consonant sounds in terms of the **place of articulation** gives more information about what the various articulators actually do. The term 'bilabial', for example, indicates that both lips are used to form a closure. For a general description of places of articulation, see page 6.

With regard to the **force of articulation**, the following terms are used: **fortis** or strong, and **lenis** or weak. In spoken English, 'fortis' happens to equate with unvoiced sounds, which require a more forcefully expelled airstream than 'lenis' sounds, which in English happen to be voiced. As far as English consonants are concerned, the distinction is most useful when it comes to distinguishing between sounds that are articulated in essentially the same way, one using the voice, the other not. An example pair is /p/

(unvoiced, and fortis) and /b/ (voiced, and lenis). Most teachers (and students) find the terms 'unvoiced' and 'voiced' more memorable, and so we will use these as the main way of distinguishing between such pairs of sounds. As suggested in Chapter 1, the difference between unvoiced and voiced sounds can be felt by touching your Adam's apple while speaking. You will feel vibration for the voiced sounds only.

At times, certain voiced sounds may be devoiced, like the /d/ at the end of *hard* /hɑːd/, for example, where the voicing is not so apparent. This is useful factual knowledge, but as an allophone (i.e. a variation of a sound which does not lead to a different word being produced), it is not so important for classroom teaching. The sounds and phonemic symbols we will consider represent, in reality, a family of possible variations.

The tables on the following pages are similar to those in the previous chapter on vowels, except that the pictures show the positions taken by the various articulators when these sounds are produced. 'Pairs' of sounds are shown together. Unvoiced sounds like /p/ are shown on a grey background. Voiced sounds like /b/ are shown on a white background.

(You may find it useful to refer back to the table of consonant phonemes in Chapter 1, page 7, and also to the learners' reference chart of English sounds, page 143. All of the sounds and example words are on the CD. The languages which are listed in shorthand are explained on page 30.)

Plosives

Plosives occur when a complete closure is made somewhere in the vocal tract. Air pressure increases behind the closure, and is then released 'explosively'. Plosive sounds are also sometimes referred to as **stops**.

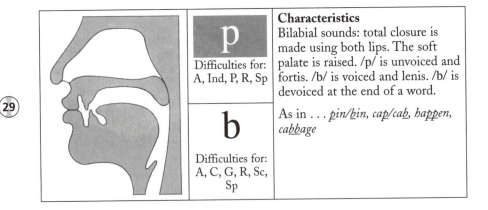

	p Difficulties for: A, Ind, P, R, Sp	**Characteristics** Bilabial sounds: total closure is made using both lips. The soft palate is raised. /p/ is unvoiced and fortis. /b/ is voiced and lenis. /b/ is devoiced at the end of a word.
	b Difficulties for: A, C, G, R, Sc, Sp	As in . . . *pin/bin, cap/cab, happen, cabbage*

48

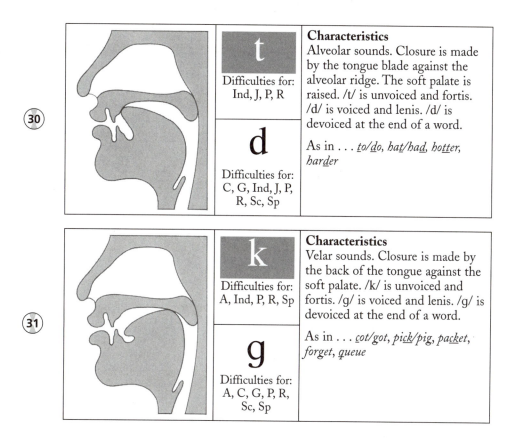

(30)

	Characteristics
t Difficulties for: Ind, J, P, R	Alveolar sounds. Closure is made by the tongue blade against the alveolar ridge. The soft palate is raised. /t/ is unvoiced and fortis. /d/ is voiced and lenis. /d/ is devoiced at the end of a word.
d Difficulties for: C, G, Ind, J, P, R, Sc, Sp	As in . . . _to_/_do_, ha_t_/ha_d_, ho_tt_er, har_d_er

(31)

	Characteristics
k Difficulties for: A, Ind, P, R, Sp	Velar sounds. Closure is made by the back of the tongue against the soft palate. /k/ is unvoiced and fortis. /g/ is voiced and lenis. /g/ is devoiced at the end of a word.
g Difficulties for: A, C, G, P, R, Sc, Sp	As in . . . _c_ot/_g_ot, pi_ck_/pi_g_, pa_ck_et, for_g_et, _q_ueue

Affricates

Affricates occur when a complete closure is made somewhere in the mouth, and the soft palate is raised. Air pressure increases behind the closure, and is then released more slowly than in plosives.

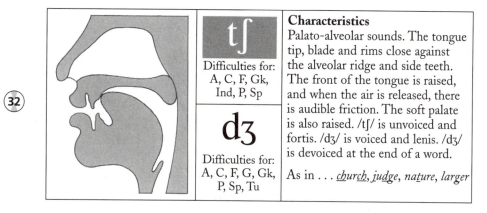

(32)

	Characteristics
tʃ Difficulties for: A, C, F, Gk, Ind, P, Sp	Palato-alveolar sounds. The tongue tip, blade and rims close against the alveolar ridge and side teeth. The front of the tongue is raised, and when the air is released, there is audible friction. The soft palate is also raised. /tʃ/ is unvoiced and fortis. /dʒ/ is voiced and lenis. /dʒ/ is devoiced at the end of a word.
dʒ Difficulties for: A, C, F, G, Gk, P, Sp, Tu	As in . . . _ch_ur_ch_, _j_u_dg_e, na_t_ure, lar_g_er

49

Fricatives

Fricatives occur when two vocal organs come close enough together for the movement of air to be heard between them.

f

Difficulties for:
J

v

Difficulties for:
A, C, G, Ind, J,
Sp, Tu

Characteristics
Labio-dental sounds. The lower lip makes light contact with the upper teeth. The soft palate is raised. /f/ is unvoiced and fortis. /v/ is voiced and lenis. /v/ is devoiced at the end of a word.

As in . . . *fan/van, hoof, hooves, cafe, cover, phase, above*

θ

Difficulties for: A, C, F, G, Ind, It, J, P, R, Sc, Tu

ð

Difficulties for:
A, C, F, G, Ind, It, J, P, R, Sc, Tu

Characteristics
Dental sounds. The tongue tip makes light contact with the back of the top, front teeth. Or, tongue tip may protrude between upper and lower teeth. The soft palate is raised. /θ/ is unvoiced and fortis. /ð/ is voiced and lenis. /ð/ is devoiced at the end of a word.

As in . . . *think, the, bath, bathe, mathematics, father*

s

Difficulties for:
J

z

Difficulties for:
A, C, F, G, Gk,
Ind, It, J, P, R, Sc,
Sp, Tu

Characteristics
Alveolar sounds. The tongue blade makes light contact with the alveolar ridge. The soft palate is raised. /s/ is unvoiced and fortis. /z/ is voiced and lenis. /z/ is devoiced at the end of a word.

As in . . . *sue/zoo, this, these, icy, lazy*

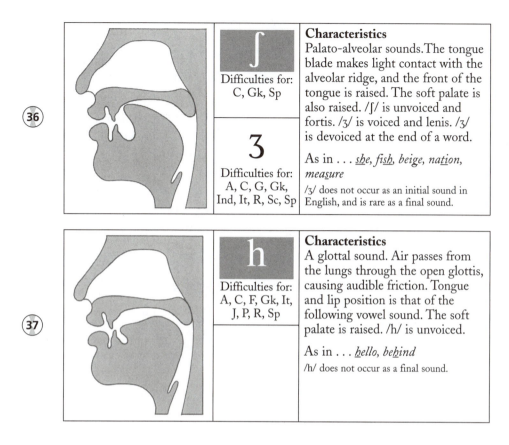

Characteristics

Palato-alveolar sounds. The tongue blade makes light contact with the alveolar ridge, and the front of the tongue is raised. The soft palate is also raised. /ʃ/ is unvoiced and fortis. /ʒ/ is voiced and lenis. /ʒ/ is devoiced at the end of a word.

As in . . . *she, fish, beige, nation, measure*

/ʒ/ does not occur as an initial sound in English, and is rare as a final sound.

ʃ

Difficulties for:
C, Gk, Sp

ʒ

Difficulties for:
A, C, G, Gk, Ind, It, R, Sc, Sp

Characteristics

A glottal sound. Air passes from the lungs through the open glottis, causing audible friction. Tongue and lip position is that of the following vowel sound. The soft palate is raised. /h/ is unvoiced.

As in . . . *hello, behind*

/h/ does not occur as a final sound.

h

Difficulties for:
A, C, F, Gk, It, J, P, R, Sp

Nasals

Nasal sounds occur when a complete closure is made somewhere in the mouth, the soft palate is lowered, and air escapes through the nasal cavity.

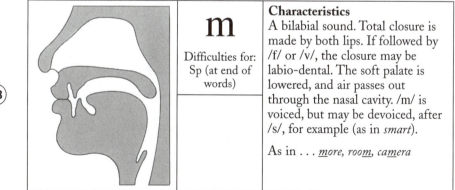

Characteristics

A bilabial sound. Total closure is made by both lips. If followed by /f/ or /v/, the closure may be labio-dental. The soft palate is lowered, and air passes out through the nasal cavity. /m/ is voiced, but may be devoiced, after /s/, for example (as in *smart*).

As in . . . *more, room, camera*

m

Difficulties for:
Sp (at end of words)

	n Difficulties for: C	**Characteristics** An alveolar sound. The tongue blade closes against the alveolar ridge, and the rims of the tongue against the side teeth. If followed by /f/ or /v/, the closure may be labio-dental, or bilabial if followed by /p/ or /b/. The soft palate is lowered, and air passes out through the nasal cavity. /n/ is voiced, but may be devoiced, after /s/, for example (as in *snow*). As in . . . *no, on, infant, know*

(39)

	ŋ Difficulties for: A, F, G, Gk, It, R, Tu	**Characteristics** A velar sound. The back of the tongue closes against the soft palate. The closure is further forward if it follows on from a front vowel (compare *sing* and *bang*). The soft palate is lowered, and air passes out through the nasal cavity. /ŋ/ is voiced. As in . . . *sing, sink, singing, sinking* /ŋ/ does not occur as an initial sound.

(40)

Lateral
The lateral is so called because, in this sound, the airflow is around the sides of the tongue.

	l Difficulties for: C, J, P	**Characteristics** A lateral sound. A partial closure is made by the blade of the tongue against the alveolar ridge. Air is able to flow around the sides of the tongue. The soft palate is raised. /l/ is voiced. As in . . . *live, pool, pulling*

(41)

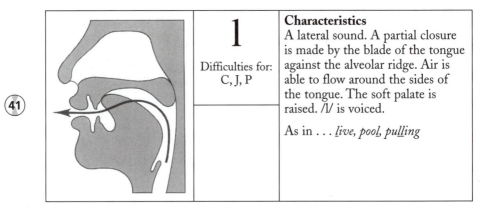

Alveolar closure with the tip of the tongue gives 'clear' *l*, as in *live*. This occurs before vowel sounds. After vowel sounds, (as in *pool*), before consonants (as in *help*), the back of the tongue is raised towards the soft palate, giving 'dark' *l* (an allophone).

Approximants

Approximants occur when one articulator moves close to another, but not close enough to cause friction or to stop the airflow. Note that /w/ and /j/ are sometimes referred to as 'semi-vowels'. This is because they are made without a restriction to the airflow, unlike the other consonants. But they act in a consonant-like way; we say *an apple*, but we say *a pear*, *a watermelon* and *a yam*. All three approximants are important linking sounds in connected speech (see Chapter 7).

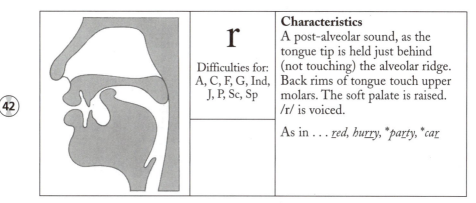

42

	r	**Characteristics**
		A post-alveolar sound, as the tongue tip is held just behind (not touching) the alveolar ridge. Back rims of tongue touch upper molars. The soft palate is raised. /r/ is voiced.
	Difficulties for: A, C, F, G, Ind, J, P, Sc, Sp	
		As in . . . <u>r</u>ed, hu<u>rr</u>y, *pa<u>r</u>ty, *ca<u>r</u>

*pronounced in these positions in rhotic accents (see page 111).

43

	j	**Characteristics**
		A palatal semi-vowel. The tongue is in the position of a close front vowel (similar to /ɪ/). The soft palate is raised. The sound glides quickly to the following vowel. /j/ is voiced.
	Difficulties for: Sp	
		As in . . . <u>y</u>es, <u>y</u>oung, <u>u</u>sual, fe<u>w</u>, q<u>ue</u>ue, ed<u>u</u>cate, s<u>u</u>it
		/j/ does not occur as a final sound.

44

	w	**Characteristics**
		A labio-velar semi-vowel. The tongue is in the position of a close back vowel (similar to /ʊ/). The soft palate is raised. The sound glides quickly to the following vowel. /w/ is voiced.
	Difficulties for: G, Ind, R, Sc, Sp, Tu	
		As in . . . <u>w</u>ood, <u>w</u>alk, <u>w</u>et, <u>wh</u>eat, hall<u>w</u>ay
		/w/ does not occur as a final sound.

Raising awareness of consonant sounds

Teachers focus on individual sounds usually as a response to a communicative difficulty which arises, or because they are an integral feature of the language being taught. Teachers should always integrate pronunciation aspects into lesson planning and language analysis, in order to raise students' general awareness. One of the best methods of helping students to master pronunciation in the classroom remains that of drilling, the repetition of the sound giving learners the opportunity to practise the correct movements of their speech organs for themselves. This, combined with 'learner-friendly' explanations of the movements, can be very effective in raising awareness of how sounds are produced.

Using diagrams and 'learner-friendly' explanations

The articulation of consonants is easier to describe than that of vowel sounds. With vowels we are attempting to describe the movement of the tongue within a space, which is extremely difficult. With consonants, however, we can talk about the parts of the mouth and throat which touch, and how they restrict, interrupt or divert the airflow.

The diagrams and tables earlier in this chapter can have their place in helping to show students how consonants are produced, but it would be unwise to assume that they are self-explanatory, and so clarification is necessary, using terms your students can understand. Telling your students that they should be using a voiced labio-dental fricative /v/ rather than a voiced bilabial plosive /b/, is unlikely to be the best approach (unless, of course, they happen to be experts in phonetics!). Instead, you could show your students a diagram and point out the following:

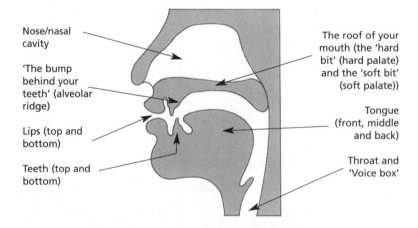

Nose/nasal cavity

'The bump behind your teeth' (alveolar ridge)

Lips (top and bottom)

Teeth (top and bottom)

The roof of your mouth (the 'hard bit' (hard palate) and the 'soft bit' (soft palate))

Tongue (front, middle and back)

Throat and 'Voice box'

Using 'easy' terms, you can more than adequately describe the range of possibilities. Rather than describing /v/ as a 'voiced labio-dental fricative', therefore, use 'learner-friendly' explanations to describe how to make the sound. For example, you could show students how to pronounce /v/ by demonstrating, and describing as follows: 'Touch your top teeth with your bottom lip, and breathe out, using your voice'. For /f/, the same description can be used, except that the instruction would be '... and breathe out, but don't use your voice'.

Teachers of course need to grade their language according to the level of the class (you can afford to be a bit more 'technical' with higher level students). The following table gives some suggested ways of explaining how to form the consonant sounds:

Sounds	Learner-friendly explanations
p b	Put your lips together. Try to breathe out, but don't let the air escape. Release the air suddenly. Don't use your voice. Try again, and add your voice.
t d	Put your tongue against the hard bump behind your teeth. Try to breathe out, but don't let the air escape. Release the air suddenly. Don't use your voice. Try again, and add your voice.
k g	Put the back of your tongue against (the soft bit of) the roof of your mouth. Try to breathe out, but don't let the air escape. Release the air suddenly. Don't use your voice. Try again, and add your voice.
f v	Touch your top teeth with your bottom lip, and breathe out. Don't use your voice. Hold the sound, and add your voice.
θ ð	Put the front of your tongue against the back of your top teeth. Let the air pass through as you breathe out. Don't use your voice. Hold the sound, and add your voice.
s z	Put the front of your tongue lightly against the bump behind your teeth. Let the air pass through as you breathe out. Don't use your voice. Hold the sound, and add your voice.
ʃ ʒ	Put the front of your tongue against the bump behind your teeth. Let the air pass through as you breathe out, making an /s/ sound. Now move your tongue slightly back. Don't use your voice. Hold the sound, and add your voice.
h	Open your mouth and breathe out. Don't use your voice, but try to make a noise.
m	Put your lips together. Use your voice, and let the air escape through your nose.
n	Put the front of your tongue against the bump behind your teeth. Use your voice, and let the air escape through your nose.
ŋ	Put the back of your tongue against the roof of your mouth. Use your voice, and let the air escape through your nose.
l	Put the front of your tongue against the bump behind your teeth. Use your voice, and let the air pass out of your mouth.
r	Point the front of your tongue towards the roof of your mouth. Use your voice.
j	Make the sound /iː/, followed by the sound /ə/. Now put them together, and keep the sound short.
w	Make the sound /uː/, followed by the sound /ə/. Now put them together, and keep the sound short.

The above explanations can, of course, be used in conjunction with a phonemic chart. Take some time to consider the above suggestions while looking at the learners' reference chart at the back of the book (see page 143).

Other techniques can also be used to help learners articulate particular sounds. One such idea is designed to show the fortis and lenis characteristics of /p/ and /b/ respectively. A small slip of paper is dangled in front of the lips, and the two sounds are made in turn; the paper should move more with /p/, due to the greater degree of aspiration (air) involved in producing the sound. The following table gives some more suggestions:

Sounds	Ideas to help students articulate sounds
p b	Hold a small piece of paper in front of your lips. Make the sounds. The paper should move for /p/, but not for /b/.
t d k g	Hold a match or lighter in front of your face. Make the sounds. You should be able to make the flame flicker for /t/ and /k/, but less for /d/ and /g/.
f v	Hold your palm in front of your mouth. Make both sounds. You should feel some air for /f/, but less for /v/.
θ ð	Place a finger against your lips. Try to touch your finger with your tongue. Breathe out. Now add your voice. (This exaggerates the positions, but will help nonetheless.)
s z	What noise does a snake make? (/s/). Now add your voice.
ʃ ʒ	What noise do you make if you want someone to be quiet? (Show 'Shh . . .' gesture if necessary.) Now add your voice.
h	Hold your palm in front of your mouth. Open your mouth and breathe out. Don't use your voice, try to make sure you can feel the air on your palm.
m	Link this with 'liking something' (e.g. food, as in *Mmm, nice*).
n	Use a word as an example, with /n/ as the last sound. Hold the sound, and get students to copy.
ŋ	Use '-ing' words as examples (e.g. *singing*).
l	Use repeated syllables, as in *lalalalala*.
r	Point your tongue towards the roof of your mouth, but don't let the tip touch. Breathe out, using your voice, and hold the sound for as long as you can.
j	Smile, and say /iː/. Now quickly say /ə/. Say the two together, and keep it short.
w	What shape is your mouth if you are going to whistle? Now use your voice, and say /wə/. Also try /wəwæwiːwɑːwuː/ etc., to practise using different vowels after /w/.

You may or may not feel comfortable using some of these ideas with your class; if in doubt, the best advice is not to do it, but devise your own alternative to suit your classroom manner and style. These are all only suggestions.

Some of the suggestions in the table above can also be used for other sounds (the 'palm in front of your mouth' idea not only works for /f/ and /v/, but also works equally well for /p/ and /b/, for example). As with vowels, teachers should use a phonemic chart to facilitate the study and practice of particular sounds, and they may find it necessary at times to use a combination of the above ideas, and the learner-friendly explanations, and the chart.

It can also help to associate sounds with pictures of objects or actions which include the sound (e.g. a pen for /p/ and a bell for /b/), but bear in mind that if students are already in the habit of mispronouncing these words, the difficulty can remain unaffected by this pictorial approach.

How to refer to the consonants
There is also the question of what to 'call' the consonants when discussing them with students. With vowels, it is easier, in the sense that you can say 'the /æ/ sound' or 'the /ɪ/ sound', or simply use the sounds themselves as names. Some teachers 'name' voiceless plosive, fricative and affricate sounds with the addition of /ə/; thus, /p/ is named as /pə/, /f/ as /fə/, /tʃ/ as /tʃə/, and so on. However, if they are trying to make the point about voicelessness, then this point may well be lost by using such a naming system, as the voice has to be used in order to produce /ə/. The system makes sense if one is dealing with voiced sounds, as the voiced nature of vowels chimes well with the voicing of the consonants, and there is no confusion.

So, for voiceless plosive and affricate sounds, for example, it is better to use a <u>whispered</u> /ə/ after the sound, so that the whole remains voiceless, preserving the point one is trying to make. It can then be easily shown that pairs of phonemes can be made for which articulation is essentially the same, apart from the presence or absence of voicing.

Voiceless fricative sounds can simply be held, and the addition of the voice can show a transition from one sound to its 'pair' (e.g. from /f/ to /v/, or /s/ to /z/). Nasal sounds can be held too, as can /l/ and /r/. The system described above is used on the CD.

Always aim to be consistent with your students in how you refer to the sounds. Using the 'naming' system described above will help to raise your students' awareness of how the sounds actually function within words.

Consonant clusters and other sound difficulties
Consonant clusters (consonant sounds which occur together, as in *matchbox* /ˈmætʃbɒks/) can provide many difficulties for learners, particularly when the cluster in question is not possible in L1. English words can have up to three consonants together at the beginning (as in *scratch* /skrætʃ/ and *splash* /splæʃ/) and up to four at the end (as in *sixths* /sɪksθs/ or *glimpsed* /glɪmpst/).

Japanese, by contrast, has very few clusters, and consonant (C) and vowel (V) sounds tend to alternate (CVC). Putting consonants together may well prove difficult, and Japanese learners may tend to insert a vowel sound into a consonant cluster, and add a vowel at the end of a word, resulting in realisations such as /ˈjesʊpʊˈriːzɒ/ for *Yes, please*. (The example also highlights the /l/ /r/ difficulty which many Japanese learners experience.)

In Spanish, the cluster /sp/ does not occur at the beginning of a word (as in English words such as *Spain*, *spouse*, *spout* and *spot*). Speakers will tend to insert an /e/ before /sp/ (and /st/ and /sk/, for that matter) as they do in L1, leading to pronunciations like /eˈspeɪn/, /eˈspɒt/, and so on. Speakers of other L1s will also bring habits across into English, or find particular clusters difficult.

As clusters are a common feature of English, they will come up very often in class, whether this be within an item of vocabulary, or in the juxtaposition of sounds when practising a structure (for example, as in *He's taller than them* /ˌhiːzˈtɔːlədənˈðem/).

Aside from drilling these difficult sounds, there are various other ideas the teacher can try out. Some clusters benefit from repetition of the sounds which occur together; for example, a student having difficulty with /sp/ might be asked to say /spspspspspsp/. This helps the student avoid the tendency to insert a vowel, and to get used to the physical feeling of putting these sounds together, which will often be very unfamiliar to the student. One can then tie the sounds in with 'familiar' words which include the cluster (such as *wasps*, or *crisps*) and which can then be included in activities and drills.

Teachers can also try isolating the clustered sounds. The word or utterance can be written on the board, in phonemic script, and students are asked to repeat the sounds slowly. For example, in the utterance used above, *He's taller than them*, you can isolate and practise /zt/ and /nð/. Hold the first sound, and then move to the second and get your students to do the same. Doing this will again help your students to get the feel of putting these sounds together.

Other sound difficulties and transferences from L1 can, of course, also cause difficulties. Possible productive difficulties are noted in the tables earlier in this chapter. Sometimes the difficulties may be due to the absence of a phoneme in L1: Italian, for example, does not have /ʒ/, and so, understandably, Italians may have difficulties with this phoneme in English.

Sometimes the difficulty is a little more complex: for example, in German, the written letter 'w' is pronounced as /v/, leading to pronunciations like /vaɪn/, for *wine*; occasionally the reverse happens, and *very* might become /ˈweriː/. To add to the complication, the letter 'v' is pronounced as /f/ in German.

Sample lessons   The activities in the following sample lessons can be used in various ways, whether for raising awareness of a pronunciation issue, or as practice of a point which has been investigated and explained in a lesson. You will also notice that some of the activities might equally well be used for practising vowels, and some necessarily include study and practice of both vowels and consonants. This reflects the nature of what goes on in the classroom; often teachers will necessarily be dealing with vowels and consonants together. All these sample lessons are Practice lessons, in the terms defined on page 14.

Lesson 1: 'Hangman': Consonant and vowel sounds (All levels)

Lesson type: Practice

The teacher demonstrates the game by doing an example on the board with the whole class. The game is played just like the normal 'Hangman' game, where players try to guess a word by suggesting letters it might contain. In this version, however, they nominate phonemes. For each 'wrong' guess made (i.e. the sound suggested is not contained in the word) a line is drawn on the board/page and these lines make up the form of a gallows with a 'stick-man' hanging from it. (See below. The origin of the game is obscure!) A correct guess is acknowledged by writing the phoneme in its correct place within the word. Wrong guesses can also be noted, so that they are not repeated.

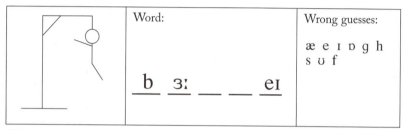

(The required word is *birthday*.)

The game is slightly more complicated than traditional 'Hangman', because when using letters, there are only 26 to choose from, whereas there are 44 phonemes. After the game has been demonstrated to the whole class, students can play their own games in pairs or small groups. The game can be made competitive if you wish, through awarding points for each word successfully guessed, but it does not need to be. Students can choose words at random, for general practice, or choose ones which have been studied recently. Alternatively, the teacher can also suggest particular words, in order to direct the practice towards particular phonemes. The game can be played between individuals, or in teams.

Lesson 2: 'I'm going to the party': Particular consonant sounds (All levels)

Lesson type: Practice

The idea of this game is for students to guess which consonant is held in common between words brought up within a stylised sentence; the sentence is *I've got a _____ , and I'm going to the party* (or you can make up your own suitable sentence). The word which students insert into the gap includes a target phoneme: students have to work out what this phoneme is as the game progresses. The target phoneme is chosen by the student who starts the game, or can be whispered or otherwise indicated to him/her by the teacher, if you wish to work on a particular sound.

The teacher sets the activity up by eliciting three recently studied items of vocabulary which happen to share a consonant phoneme, and also elicits that this is what the words have in common. She then briefly explains the game, and introduces the sentence (*I've got a _____, and I'm going to the party*). One student starts the game, saying for example, *I've got a cap* /kæp/, *and I'm going to the party*. (Let's assume the target phoneme is /p/.) The second student tries to guess what the target phoneme is, saying for example, *I've got a car* /kɒː/, *and I'm going to the party*. The student here has wrongly assumed that the target phoneme is /k/, and so the student who began will say *No, you aren't*. The third person might guess correctly that the phoneme is /p/, and say *I've got a parrot* /'pærət/, *and I'm going to the party*. The first student will then reply *Yes, you are*, as the target has been correctly guessed. Occasionally people will get it right without realising why!

The game progresses until everyone has guessed the target phoneme, and includes it in their sentence. It is best played in groups of five or six, so that students don't have to wait too long for their turn. Teachers may also need to be ready to chip in with suggestions, in order to keep the game moving.

Lesson 3: Phonemic word search: Consonant and vowel sounds (All levels)

Lesson type: Practice
Materials: Word search grid

This activity is a familiar one, where students search a grid for 'hidden' words, but with the words written phonemically. Words may appear horizontally, vertically, diagonally and also in reverse. Although they take some preparation, it is worth spending some time devising them. It is useful to have a few larger ones for general practice, and smaller ones which can be tailored for particular classes, either to practise particular phonemes, or to work on recently covered vocabulary. The activity can also be used to introduce new words, particularly if tied to a subject area; for example, if students know that they are looking for 'vegetables', but don't know the word /'kæbɪdʒ/ (*cabbage*), finding it in the grid can neatly prompt the word for further work and practice. The following sample is a 'vegetable' grid.

j	s	w	iː	t	k	ɔː	n
ə	aʊ	l	f	ɪ	l	ɒ	k
t	ʊ	k	s	p	r	aʊ	t
ə	k	æ	r	ə	t	n	aʊ
m	k	b	v	ŋ	ɜː	b	r
ɑː	h	ɪ	z	ʊ	n	iː	p
t	b	dʒ	f	iː	ɪ	n	f
əʊ	t	eɪ	t	ə	p	z	ə

(The words hidden in the grid are *sweetcorn, cauliflower, sprout, carrot, potato, pea, tomato, cabbage, turnip, bean*.)

The teacher demonstrates the activity by showing students the grid (for example, on a handout, or on the overhead projector) and asks them to find a word. When one student offers a suggestion, the teacher makes sure that all the students can see the word. She then tells the students that the words can be found going in all directions (though grids can be made less complex if you wish) and sets a time limit for the activity. Students can work on their handouts singly or in pairs. As a follow up activity they can be asked to devise their own grids; this can be a marvellous way of focusing attention on phonemes. Students can do this in small groups, and their grids can be given to other groups to solve.

Lesson 4: Advertising slogans: Particular consonant sounds (All levels)

Lesson type: Practice
Materials: advertisements from magazines or newspapers/video of television adverts

The teacher shows students some popular or well-known advertisements from newspapers or magazines, or videotaped from the television, which include a catchy slogan used to advertise the particular product. She then asks the students to think up a new slogan for one of the products, but using the phoneme which the product's name begins with as many times as possible. Students are given a short time to do this, and suggestions are elicited from the class and written up on the board. If the suggestions don't particularly work, the teacher can offer one or two of her own. The teacher then tells the students that their task is to think up a product which might be advertised using a slogan; the slogan must aim to include the target phoneme as many times as possible. Here, a particular sound may be worked on, or the teacher may set phoneme targets for particular students, depending on the variety of 'difficult' sounds the teacher wishes to work on. Slogans (and accompanying pictures) can be drawn on paper, and 'advertised' on the wall, or put up on the board.

A group of Japanese students, whose target phoneme was /r/, produced the following suggestion:

A variation would be to use the activity to work on the contrast between two sounds which are causing difficulty. Here, the sounds being worked on are /w/ and /v/, which can cause difficulties for German speakers:

> # Vera's Wonderful
> # Wedding Videos

To add to the difficulty of the activity, students might also be asked to give a short 'sales talk' about their product, again the idea being to include as many examples of the target phoneme(s) as possible. A similar exercise can be done with invented newspaper headlines.

Lesson 5: Running dictation: Particular consonant/vowel sounds (All levels)

Lesson type: Practice
Materials: prepared texts for dictation

In this activity, pairs or teams compete to dictate a short passage, or a series of words (depending on which sounds, lexis or grammar the teacher wishes to work on). He puts these up on the wall of the classroom, or in another suitable place the students can get to easily. The game is best played in pairs.

The first member of each pair runs to the wall, and tries to memorise the contents of the dictation sheet as fast as possible. She then runs back to her team-mate, and dictates what she can remember. Her partner attempts to write it down in phonemic script. At various points, the teacher claps, or gives some other agreed signal for the pair or team members to change roles.

The task can integrate work on pronunciation, grammar and lexis; the teacher can change the emphasis placed on pronunciation issues by doing any of the following:

- the target text is written in phonemic script and must also be written down in phonemic script, or
- the target text is written in phonemic script but must be written down using the alphabet, or
- the target text is written normally, but must be written down in phonemic script.

Further ideas for activities

'Sound chain'

This activity is useful for working on initial clusters of two or more consonants. Starting with a given word (which can be suggested either by the teacher or by the first student in the chain), students think of a word which includes, in its own initial cluster, one of the sounds which appears in the previous word. For example:

green /gri:n/ *brick* /brɪk/ *blue* /blu:/ *play* /pleɪ/ *flower* /flaʊə/ *friend* /frend/

The activity requires good knowledge of the consonant phonemes, and a good vocabulary, too. It is best played with Intermediate level students and above who are reasonably familiar with phonemic transcription. If you feel it will help make the task more achievable, let students refer to a phonemic chart while doing the activity, to help jog their memories; don't, however, let this slow the activity down too much. It may be an idea to set a 'thinking time' limit. You can make the game co-operative or competitive, as you and your students prefer, and it can be played in pairs or small teams or as a whole class.

'Tongue-twisters'

These were mentioned as a general idea in Chapter 2, but can be particularly useful for working on difficult consonant phonemes. Well-known examples are things like *Around the rugged rock, the ragged rascal ran* (useful for practising /r/) and *She sells sea shells on the sea shore* (which might be used for contrasting the articulations of /s/ and /ʃ/). Bear in mind, though, that the very nature of tongue-twisters means that native speakers find them difficult to say also, and that you are duty-bound to explain what a *ragged rascal* is! Try making up your own, or get students to write them. Here are some real examples produced by students of different nationalities:

Ban vans! Ban vans! Ban vans! (Spanish speakers, practising /b/ and /v/).
Try Gerry's Charming German Cherry Gin (German speakers, practising /dʒ/ and /tʃ/).
This theatre, that theatre, this theatre, that theatre (French speakers, practising /θ/ and /ð/).

In order to write their own tongue-twisters, students need of course to have an awareness of which sounds cause them difficulty! The teacher can suggest these if necessary, but needs to be careful to choose phonemes which actually cause difficulties. You may also need to suggest creative ideas if your students find the task too taxing. Tongue-twisters need not be linguistically complex; the first example above only contains two words, yet adequately practises the contrast between /b/ and /v/, and the third one only has three words, and does its job admirably.

Fill the grid

Draw a grid on the board (see the example on page 64), or on an overhead projector. Students (or teams) take it in turns to suggest one phoneme at a time, gradually building up the number of phonemes on the grid, until it is possible to form words going either across or down (or in other directions, if you want to increase the number of possibilities; this also increases the complexity of the activity, however).

Students nominate a square, and decide which phoneme they want to put in it. For example, the first student might say 'A3, /p/', and the teacher or the student can put the phoneme in the relevant square. The next person might put an /e/ in G8, for example, and so on. Let's say that an /e/ appears at some point in B3; the next person can put a /n/ in C3, earning three points for the number of phonemes used in the word. The game carries on until an agreed target number of points has been accumulated by one of the players or teams, or until an agreed time limit has expired. A grid in progress might look something like this:

	A	B	C	D	E	F	G	H	I	J
1										
2								aʊ		
3	p	e	n							
4						h	ʊ			
5						e				
6		ð				l				
7	tʃ	eə		s		əʊ				
8							e			
9										
10	t	ʃ					θ			

The teacher can include a few strategically placed phonemes to help the game get off to a good start.

'Phoneme and vocabulary exerciser'

Choose a sound or sounds you want to concentrate on; for a multilingual class you could choose a suitable sound for each student, and for a monolingual class you might be able to choose a sound for the whole group of students.

Then choose various categories (see the table below). Students have to give at least one word per category which starts with the 'target' phoneme. You can vary the instructions (for example, the words might simply have to include the target sound rather than start with it), and the activity can be done as a race against the clock, as a collaborative exercise, individually, as a class, or in teams. The examples below have been produced by learners having difficulty with /p/. The activity might equally well be used for working with vowel sounds.

Food	Place	Part of Body	Animal	Colour	Verb
peas	Poland	pupil	pig	purple	press

Do make sure, of course, that the task is achievable; try it out yourself, and see if you can think of a word for each category that you might reasonably expect your students to be able to offer in class! If not, then you will need to change the categories accordingly.

'Sound race'

This is similar to the above activity, but it gives students more freedom of choice over which words they can bring up. A 'difficult' sound (or consonant cluster) is written phonemically on the board. Teams or individuals compete to see how many words they can think of within a given time limit which include the target sound. To vary the degree of difficulty, instructions might be that the words must be two syllables or more, or that the students have to provide a certain number of words with the sound at the beginning, middle and end.

'Who am I? What's my line? What am I?'
This is a version of an old party game, which can be adapted to practise particular sounds and items of lexis. Stick a piece of paper on students' backs or foreheads, with the name of a famous, modern or historical figure written in phonemic script on each one. Bear in mind the age, background etc. of your students in deciding which names to use. Students can ask questions in order to find out the name they have been given ('Am I a woman?', 'Am I an actor?', etc). When they think they know, ask them to write the name in phonemic script on the board, and see if it matches with what is on their sticker. Bear in mind if you use 'foreign' names, that your students might not pronounce *Leonardo da Vinci*, for example, in the same way that you do!

Conclusions

In this chapter we have:
- considered the characteristics of the consonant sounds. Consonant sounds can be described in terms of the manner, place and force of articulation. Sounds may also be 'voiced' or 'unvoiced'. We have primarily thought about manner, place and the presence or absence of voicing.
- studied the characteristics of the consonant sounds and listed first languages whose speakers may have productive difficulties with these sounds in English.
- thought about some 'learner-friendly' ways of describing the consonants, and thought about some techniques to help individuals form consonants which they have difficulty with.
- considered ways of raising awareness of consonant sounds in the classroom, and been reminded again that teachers should always aim to integrate pronunciation work into their teaching.
- considered a variety of classroom activities for focusing on consonant sounds in the classroom.

Looking ahead

In Chapter 5 we will:
- consider how syllables may be stressed or unstressed, and the implications this can have for meaning.
- look at how stress and unstress can also affect the qualities of certain phonemes.
- introduce the idea of levels of stress.
- consider further the role of drilling.
- think about how to integrate work on stress into teaching, and look at some activities for working on stress in the classroom.
- start investigating the links between stress and intonation.

In Chapter 6 we will:
- look at intonation in more detail.

Word and sentence stress

- **What is word stress?**
- **What is unstress?**
- **Rules of word stress**
- **Levels of stress**
- **Sentences: Stress timing and syllable timing**
- **Sentence stress and tonic syllables**
- **Sentence stress and weak forms**
- **Raising awareness of word and sentence stress**
- **Sample lessons**
  - **Lesson 1: Find a partner: Stress patterns**
  - **Lesson 2: Three little words: Contrastive stress**
  - **Lesson 3: Misunderstanding dialogues: Contrastive stress**
  - **Lesson 4: Listening and transcribing: Stress placement in a short monologue**
  - **Lesson 5: Categorisation: Word stress**
- **Further ideas for activities**
- **Putting sentence stress into perspective**

What is word stress?

Try saying the following words to yourself: *qualify, banana, understand*. All of them have three identifiable syllables, and one of the syllables in each word will sound louder than the others: so, we get *QUAlify, baNAna* and *underSTAND*. (The syllables indicated in capitals are the stressed syllables.) Each stressed syllable, in a word in isolation, also has a change in the **pitch**, or the level of the speaker's voice, and the vowel sound in that syllable is lengthened.

Stress can fall on the first, middle or last syllables of words, as is shown here:

Ooo	oOo	ooO
SYLlabus	enGAGEment	usheRETTE
SUBstitute	baNAna	kangaROO
TECHnical	phoNEtic	underSTAND

45

66

The words in the first group (Ooo) are all stressed on the first syllable, the words in the second group are stressed on the second syllable, and those in the third group are stressed on the third syllable.

If you have any difficulty initially in recognising where the stress falls, try making the word in question the last word in a short sentence, and saying it over a few times (for example, *It's in the syllabus*; *He had a prior engagement*; *I don't understand*). Listen to the examples on the CD. This should help you to ascertain the pattern for the word you are considering. Another idea is to say the word in question as though you have been completely taken by surprise, or are taken aback by the mere mention of the idea (for example, *SYLLabus? baNAna? kangaROO?*).

(46)

(47)

Some find it relatively easy to spot stresses, and others will take time to be able to do so consistently. Whichever group you fall into, you need to be aware of stress, and to deal with it specifically in class. If students are first made aware of stress, and then given practice in identifying stressed syllables, they will be better able to work towards using it appropriately when speaking.

What is unstress? In order for one syllable to be perceived as stressed, the syllables around it need to be unstressed. For stressed syllables, three features were identified: loudness, pitch change and a longer syllable. Unstress may be described as the absence of these.

Have another look at the groups of words in the previous table. In the word *syllabus*, we said that the first syllable was stressed. This logically implies that the final two are unstressed. Also, in the word *banana*, the first and third syllables are unstressed, and the middle one is stressed. The same applies to the other words in the table.

The idea, as we will see later, is a little simplified here, but the basic contrast between stressed and unstressed syllables is a useful concept to hold on to, and for many classroom situations, this level of detail is enough to help students towards more successful pronunciation.

On the subject of unstressed syllables, however, there are various things to notice. In Chapter 3, we considered the phoneme known as 'schwa' (the phonemic transcription is /ə/). This sound can be heard in the first syllable of *about*, in the second syllable of *paper*, and also in the third syllable of *intricate*. The table below shows the incidences of /ə/ with the corresponding written vowels underlined.

Ooo	oOo	ooO
SYLlabus	enGAGEment	usheRETTE
SUBstitute	baNAna	kangaROO
TECHnical	phoNETic	underSTAND

As mentioned in Chapter 3, /ə/ is the most commonly occurring vowel sound in English. It never appears within a stressed syllable. Schwa is by nature an unstressed sound. If you try to stress any syllable which naturally contains /ə/, you change its properties, and another phoneme is produced.

Schwa is not unique to the English language, but it is its most frequent sound. Difficulties may arise for students if this sound does not occur in their first language, or from the interference of other pronunciation rules and tendencies that they might bring over into spoken English. Perception is also crucial, in that as /ə/ is such a common feature of English, lack of awareness of its role may add to students' difficulties in understanding native speaker speech.

As can be seen from the words in the table below, /ə/ can be represented through spelling in a variety of ways. Here are some spellings, with the incidences of /ə/ underlined. Remember, though, that these may not always tally with the reader's own accent or variety of English.

(48)

> *a*, as in *arise, syllable, banana*
> *e*, as in *phenomenon, excellent and vowel*
> *i*, as in *pupil, experiment and communicate*
> *o*, as in *tomorrow, button or develop*
> *u* as in *support, bogus and difficult*

Sometimes whole syllables or word endings may be 'reduced' to /ə/, as in *butter, thorough, facilitator* and *polar*. This is common among British English accents, though not so common in US English.

(49)

At other times /ə/ is a central sound in a syllable, and several written vowels may represent the sound; this is very common in words ending in *-ous* (like *conscious* and *fictitious*). It also occurs frequently in *-al* endings (like *spatial, capital* and *topical*), in *-ion* words (like *session, pronunciation* and *attention*) and *-ate* endings (like *accurate, private* and *delicate*).

You will notice that there is one word in the table on the previous page in which /ə/ does not occur (*substitute*). It is important to remember that not <u>all</u> unstressed syllables contain /ə/, but it is our most common vowel sound.

Rules of word stress

The list opposite provides a 'rough guide' to stressed syllables. It is more accurate to see these as descriptions of tendencies rather than rules, in that they only tell us what is true most of the time, and it is always possible to find exceptions. It is not suggested that teachers simply pass on this information 'en masse' to their students: it will be of some use, and is certainly worth studying at appropriate times, but it will not always be available for students to recall and use in real-time communication.

It makes sense to use such information to help students to discover patterns which are applicable and relevant to the language they are learning at a particular time, but always bear in mind that they are rules of thumb only.

(50)

> **Core vocabulary:** Many 'everyday' nouns and adjectives of two-syllable length are stressed on the first syllable. Examples are: *SISter, BROther, MOther, WAter, PAper, TAble, COFfee, LOvely* etc.
>
> **Prefixes and suffixes:** These are not usually stressed in English. Consider: *QUIet*<u>*ly*</u>, *oRIGin*<u>*ally*</u>, *de*FECtive, and so on. (Note the exceptions, though, among prefixes, like <u>*BI*</u>*cycle* and <u>*DIS*</u>*locate*.)
>
> **Compound words:** Words formed from a combination of two words tend to be stressed on the first element. Examples are: *POSTman, NEWSpaper, TEApot* and *CROSSword*.
>
> **Words having a dual role:** In the case of words which can be used as either a noun or a verb, the noun will tend to be stressed on the first syllable (in line with the 'core vocabulary' rule above) and the verb on the last syllable (in line with the 'prefix rule'). Examples are *IMport* (n), *imPORT* (v); *REbel* (n), *reBEL* (v) and *INcrease* (n), *inCREASE* (v).

Levels of stress

So far, we have looked at syllables in terms of being either stressed or unstressed. In fact within longer words syllables can have different degrees of stress. To be more theoretically accurate, we should consider all syllables in terms of their level of stress, rather than its presence or absence, particularly when dealing with words in isolation. Different commentators have outlined up to five different levels of stress in a single word: Daniel Jones, in *An Outline of English Phonetics* cites the word *opportunity*, which has five levels of stress as seen below. '1' indicates the greatest level of stress, and '5' the least.

$$\overset{2\quad4\quad1\quad5\ 3}{/ɒpəˈtjuːnɪtiː/}$$

Jones qualified this, however, by saying that he thought that this viewpoint needed 'modification', and that here stress was affected by 'subtle degrees of vowel and consonant length, and by intonation' (1960: 247). While Jones' example seems somewhat excessive for our purposes, the existence of different levels of stress is well documented and evidenced.

Many commentators settle on a three-level distinction between primary stress, secondary stress and unstress, as seen in the following examples.

(51)

o . O ..
opportunity

O . o
telephone

O . o
substitute

However, in practical terms a two-level division (stressed or unstressed) is usually adequate for teaching purposes. Many people (including many teachers) will have difficulty in perceiving more than two levels of stress with any confidence. Two levels of stress are enough to attune learners' ears and attention to how stress acts within words and utterances.

This is not, of course, to discourage teachers from further investigations into the nature of stress at a deeper level. The deeper one's understanding of the subject matter, the better one's teaching of it is likely to be. Teachers need to be as informed as possible in order to be better able to make the decision as to what to include in lessons. If students notice or enquire about more than two levels of stress, then of course this should be acknowledged and discussed in class. The teacher must feel confident in making informed decisions about the method and content of these discussions, backed up by professional knowledge.

Sentences: Stress timing and syllable timing

It has been claimed that certain languages (for example English, Arabic and Russian) are **stress-timed**, or **isochronous** /aɪˈsɒkrənəs/. In such languages stresses occur at regular intervals within connected speech, it is claimed, and the duration of an utterance is more dependent upon the number of stresses than the number of syllables. To achieve the regular stress intervals, unstressed syllables are made shorter, and the vowels often lose their 'pure' quality, with many tending towards /ə/, and others towards /ɪ/ and /ʊ/.

Other languages (such as Japanese, French and Spanish) are said to be **syllable-timed**. In these languages there is no strong pattern of stress; syllables maintain their length, and vowels maintain their quality. Certain syllables are still stressed, of course, but not according to a regular pattern.

Isochronicity might be shown as in the following example. We start with a simple sentence; we add syllables to it on each line, but the time it takes to say the utterance remains the same.

they LIVE	in an	OLD	HOUSE
they LIVE	in a NICE	OLD	HOUSE
they LIVE	in a LOVEly	OLD	HOUSE
they've been LIVing	in a deLIGHTful	OLD	HOUSE
they've been LIVing	in a deLIGHTful	OLD	COTTage
they've been LIVing	in a deLIGHTful	vicTORian	COTTage

The occurrence of stresses remains regular, and unstressed syllables are squashed in between the stressed ones, being shorter and losing some purity of the vowel sound. If you simply tap out the rhythm it is easy to be persuaded of the validity of this idea. One can indeed say this sequence of sentences with a regular rhythm, which seems to be preserved as one adds more syllables. There is also a strong contrast between stressed and unstressed syllables.

However, consider also the speed at which you are talking by the time you get to the last utterance in the group. From slowly and deliberately in the first sentence, one moves by stages to far more rapid speech in the last line. The persuasiveness of the idea makes the evidence fit the theory, rather than the theory being supported by the evidence.

It makes more sense to imagine English described in terms of a continuum which has tendencies towards stress-timing at one end and syllable-timing at the other. A language like English has more of a tendency than some other languages to reduce vowel length and quality in unstressed syllables, and so tends towards the stress-timing end of the continuum.

So-called syllable-timed languages also reduce the length of the vowel in an unstressed syllable, though to a lesser extent, but they tend to preserve the quality of the vowel sound.

Stress timing and regular rhythms are most noticeable in highly stylised and patterned language, such as poetry or nursery rhymes. How far the phenomenon is observable in everyday speech is a matter for debate. Regularity of speech rhythm varies widely according to context, as it may bring in factors such as the relationship between the speakers, their confidence, nervousness, etc. and whether their speech is rehearsed or spontaneous, not to mention personal habits of accent, dialect and so on. As we will see in the next section too, the words and syllables which we choose to stress in connected speech are in fact dictated very much by context, and the meanings we wish to communicate when speaking.

Using language which is rhythmic and clearly patterned can, however, be very useful in the classroom, particularly for making students aware of the importance of stress (and intonation) in English, and also for highlighting weak forms and other features of connected speech.

Sentence stress and tonic syllables

The use of stress in speech helps us both deliver and understand meaning in longer utterances and it is closely linked with **intonation**. Although we will inevitably mention intonation, in this chapter we will concentrate on which syllables are stressed and why. In Chapter 6, we will look further at how intonation contributes to the meaning of what we say.

Consider the following sentence:

he LIVES in the HOUSE on the CORner.

(Capitals have not been used where they would usually occur (i.e. on *he*) in order to preserve the distinction between stressed and unstressed syllables.) The above example sentence conveys three different ideas: he resides in a particular dwelling; that dwelling is what the people involved in the conversation would consider to be a house, as opposed to a flat or a bungalow; the precise location of the house is at the junction of two or more streets, this junction being either familiar or obvious to the hearer. This gives us three **content words** (*lives*, *house* and *corner*), which convey the most important ideas in the sentence. The rest of the utterance consists of **function words**, which we need in order to make our language hold together.

The example is rather stylised, however, and glosses over what actually happens when the sentence is said in context. In order to arrive at an understanding of this, we need initially to go back to word stress.

(52) The word *corner* has two syllables, the first one being stressed, and the second one unstressed, as follows: *CORner*.

(53) If I ask you *Where is John's house?*, and it happens to be at a junction of two or more streets, that junction being either known to us both or obvious to us both, you might answer like this: *It's on the CORner.*

The first syllable of *corner* in this sentence is the **tonic syllable**. It is indicated by underlining. *Corner* is the most important word in the sentence as it effectively answers the question *Where?* The tonic syllable is the most stressed syllable in an utterance – it is generally longer, louder, and carries the main pitch movement in an utterance (in this example, the pitch of the voice falls on it).

(54) If, on the other hand, one friend asks another to confirm where John's house is, the question might be *Where did you say John lives?* In this case, a possible answer is as follows:

he LIVES in the house on the CORner.

Here, *lives* is given some stress, and so it is written in capitals. *Lives* in this sentence is the **onset syllable**, in that it establishes a pitch that stays more or less level right through to *cor-* (which is still our tonic syllable), on which it drops. That the word *house* is not stressed here tells us that this is shared knowledge between the speakers, and it is not necessary to point this out. It is possible to detect a small degree of stress on *house*, but relative to *lives* and *cor-*, it is noticeably less prominent.

The new information that is being shared between speakers determines what is the tonic syllable. Look at this example:

(55) John lives in the block of flats on the corner, doesn't he?
NO, he LIVES in the HOUSE on the corner.

Here, *lives* is again an onset syllable, but the tonic syllable is now *house*, reflecting the importance of this word within the utterance. *No* is also a tonic syllable, and is followed by a pause. While the first syllable of *corner* is stressed when the word is said on its own, here it is not given any stress, as it is knowledge already shared between the speakers.

The following example shows a similar effect:

(56) John's buying the house on the corner, isn't he?
he ALready LIVES in the house on the corner.

Within utterances, therefore, we emphasise tonic syllables in order to highlight the most significant new information. We use onset syllables to initiate a pitch which continues up to the tonic syllable. We will develop these important ideas further in Chapter 6, which takes a closer look at intonation.

With regard to sentence stress we can outline a three-stage process which enables us to say the same thing in different ways:

1 When we say words of more than one syllable in isolation we will stress one of the syllables.

2 When words are arranged together in a sentence or utterance, certain syllables will be stressed in order to convey the most important new information. This may cancel out normal word stress.

3 Intonation is used to give further subtleties of meaning to the syllables we have chosen to stress.

Speakers make certain assumptions with regard to what is old and new information, and express these by means of stress (and intonation) patterns. Hearers confirm or deny these assumptions through their reactions.

Remember also that our spoken language is not tied to sentences. When conversing, we often use incomplete sentences, phrases which would be considered ungrammatical if written down, interrupt each other, backtrack and so on. However, a study of stress within complete sentences provides a 'user-friendly' way of drawing attention to the main aspects of how we use stress in speech.

Sentence stress and weak forms

(57)

There are a large number of words in English which can have a 'full' form and a 'weak' form. For example, compare the use of the word *can* and *from* in the following sentences:

> She can /kən/ swim faster than I can /kæn/. (The first *can* is the weak form, and the second *can* is the full form.)
> She's from /frəm/ Scotland. Where are you from /frɒm/? (The first *from* is the weak form, and the second *from* is the full form.)

As these words can be pronounced differently, it is important that learners are taught the possible forms of these words when they are introduced. These words are most often the function words, filling in between content words, and making sentences 'work', grammatically.

Receptive exercises can be used to attune students' minds to the idea, and to work towards recognition of the different forms. Productive exercises can also be used to help students towards their target of pronunciation. The most frequently cited examples of these words are as outlined in the following table:

Grammatical category	Word	Full form	Weak form	Example of weak form
Verbs	am	æm	m	That's what I'm trying to say.
	are	ɑː	ə	Where are you from?
	is	ɪz	əz/z/s	Where's he from?/Where is he from?
	was	wɒz	wəz	That's where he was born.
	were	wɜː	wə	That's where my children were born.
	do	duː	də	Where do you live?
	does	dʌz	dəz	Where does he live?
	have	hæv	əv/v	He will have left by now./They've gone.
	has	hæz	həz/əz/z/s	The baby has swallowed a stone./He's gone.
	had	hæd	həd/əd/d	He had already gone./He'd already gone.
	can	kæn	kən	I'm not sure if I can lend it to you.
	could	kʊd	kəd	Well, what could I say?
	would	wʊd	wəd/əd	Well, what would you have done?
	should	ʃʊd	ʃəd/ʃd	Well, what should I have said?
Personal pronouns	you	juː	jə	How do you do?
	your	jɔː	jə	What does your boss think?
	he	hiː	hɪ/ɪ	Where does he work?
	him	hɪm	ɪm	I'll give it to him later.
	she	ʃiː	ʃɪ	She's leaving tomorrow.
	her	hɜː	hə/ə	I'll give it to her later.
	us	ʌs	əs	They'll give it to us later.
	them	ðem	ðəm	I'll give it to them later.
Prepositions	to	tuː	tə	He's already gone to work.
	at	æt	ət	He's at work, I think.
	of	ɒv	əv	That's the last of the wine!
	for	fɔː	fə	He's away for two weeks.
	from	frɒm	frəm	She comes from Scotland.
Conjunctions	and	ænd	ən/ənd	She's tall and fair.
	but	bʌt	bət	She's here, but Juan isn't.
	than	ðæn	ðən	She's older than you.
Articles	a	eɪ	ə	He's a doctor.
	an	æn	ən	She's an architect.
	the	ðiː	ðə	She's the person I told you about.
Indefinite adjectives	any	eniː	əniː/niː	Have we got any biscuits?
	some	sʌm	səm	There's some tea in the pot.
	such	sʌtʃ	sətʃ	It's not such a big deal, really.

Keep in mind when teaching weak forms that in certain positions, the full form is necessary. Also, at times, speakers may wish to emphasise function words for particular reasons:

(59)   no, I was coming FROM the station, not going TO it.

Weak forms are an important feature of ordinary, everyday speech, and students should have the opportunity of becoming attuned to them. Students should be given the opportunity to practise both strong and weak forms and receive feedback on their production from a teacher in order to be able to produce the mix of strong and weak forms correctly, if they should wish.

Raising awareness of word and sentence stress

Each time the teacher plans to introduce a new vocabulary item, it is important that he considers what the students actually need to know about the word: meaning, collocation (i.e. which other words commonly go with it), 'currency' (i.e. whether or not the word is restricted to certain situations or can be used widely), spelling and pronunciation.

With regard to pronunciation, stressed and unstressed syllables are important features. There are various ways in which the teacher can encourage a continuing awareness of stress. Receptive awareness is important, as it is through this that successful production tends to come. Choral and individual drilling of new words usefully combines receptive awareness and productive skill. While it is important for teachers to appreciate that successful repetition during drilling will not necessarily lead to continued accurate production during other practice activities, or outside the classroom, it is vital to give students this opportunity to practise.

Teachers should try drilling words in a natural manner, first. If the students are having difficulty, it is a good idea to try exaggerating the stressed syllable (though as this inevitably changes the characteristics of the phonemes involved you should always come back to the unexaggerated word once your students have got the point). Other techniques commonly employed are beating out the pattern of stress with your hand or finger, or tapping with a pen on the table, speaking or singing the stress pattern (DA da da), and so on.

Listening activities are particularly useful for helping to raise awareness of word stress. Some suggestions for these are outlined in the sample lessons.

As has been suggested throughout the book so far, pronunciation work should be seen as an integral part of what goes on in the classroom, and it is important that teachers treat it as such. With this in mind, it is important to get into the habit of indicating the stress pattern on any new words you have presented, particularly those words which you would like students to note down, remember and use.

There are several ways of indicating stress when it comes to writing a word on the board or in a handout for your students:

Circles can be written above or below the word: *syllabus*

Some teachers like to use boxes: *engagement*

You can put a mark before the stressed syllable: *ushe'rette*

Note that this is also a convention used in dictionaries, when a phonemic transcription is given alongside the particular entry: /ʌʃə'ret/

You can simply underline the stressed syllable: *tech̲nical*

Or write it in capitals: *comPUter*

Inevitably teachers tend to develop particular habits, and find themselves using one convention more than the others. It's a good idea to aim to stick with the one which comes most naturally to you, and, as with many things in teaching, aim to be both clear and consistent, so that students become familiar with your teaching habits. After a certain amount of repeated exposure to your stress-marking habits, students will know what the symbols mean, without having to ask, and students familiar with the habit can pass on their knowledge to new students, and so on.

When dealing with longer utterances and sentences, drilling is again important, and can be very useful for highlighting both stress and weak forms. With longer utterances, front or back chaining can be tried (see page 16), and 'beating' stress can also help. A little caution is advisable, however, as it is important not to 'overdo' sentence stress, in the sense of giving stress to too many elements within an utterance. By way of example, let us look again at the sentence we used earlier: *He lives in the house on the corner.* We should remember that though *lives* and *house* and *corner* may be 'content' words when the sentence is considered out of context, in reality within a conversation the sentence would have a tonic syllable, carrying a change in pitch, and being an important indicator of meaning. Drilling the sentence with an equal emphasis on all three content words, might lead to rather unnatural sounding production. Keep in mind the context in which the sentence appears, and the meaning which the sentence is trying to convey, think about where the pitch movement occurs (i.e. on the tonic syllable) and drill accordingly.

Weak forms can be isolated and drilled on their own, before being put back into the sentence or utterance. For example, in the sentence *If I'd known the answer, I would've told you*, the words *would've* can be isolated and drilled separately, if students are having difficulty with them. The whole sentence might then be drilled once more, to show again how the other language fits around it.

In raising awareness of issues relating to word and sentence stress, teachers should treat these issues as part of the language being studied. They should, for example, show students how to record stresses in their notebooks for later study which will aid students in both comprehension and language production. It is useful to use (and teach your students) questions like 'Which word is stressed?', 'Which syllable is stressed?', or 'Where does the voice go up/down?', so that you can elicit facts about the stresses in the language item you are teaching, and so that students can ask you about it, if they are not sure.

Sample lessons   In this section are some classroom activities which will help to focus attention on word and sentence stress. Some of these might be used from time to time for general awareness of the issue, and most can be adapted for use with a variety of grammatical and lexical topics.

Lesson 1: Find a partner: Stress patterns (All levels)

Lesson type: Practice
Materials: Sentence and word cards

The teacher gives half of the students a card each with a word on, and the other half a card with a sentence on. Each word card has a sentence card match, the word and sentence both having the same stress pattern. Students mingle, saying their words or sentences out loud, and, through listening, trying to find their partner. When they think they have found a partner, they check with the teacher, and if they are indeed a pair, they can sit down. Once all of the students are paired up, the pairs read out their word and sentence to the other students, who write down the stress pattern, using a small circle to represent unstressed syllables, and a large one to represent a stressed syllable, as in the following example:

Politician ooOo
It's important ooOo

No meaning relationship is implied through the pairs having the same pattern; it is simply an exercise to help students to notice the difference between stressed and unstressed syllables. Sample cards (using some job-related words) might be as follows:

Politician / It's important
Policeman / He's English
Electrician / Can I help you?
Photographer / You idiot!
Interior designer / I want to go to London

Lesson 2: Three little words: Contrastive stress (All levels)

Lesson type: Practice

This short activity provides a simple way of demonstrating the effect that a shifting tonic syllable can have on the meaning of an utterance. The teacher writes *I love you* on the board, and asks the students which syllable is stressed, eliciting that it is the word *love*. He draws a stress box over the word to show this or rewrites it in capitals. He then writes the same sentence up twice more. The students then work in pairs to see if they can work out any other possible meanings, through stressing the other words in the sentence. Suggested answers are as follows:

Sentence (meaning)
I <u>love</u> you (...and I want you to know this).
I love <u>you</u>. (I don't love her.)
<u>I</u> love you. (He doesn't!)

Those 'three little words' which carry such weight, can also carry different, and very much context-related, meanings. Of course you can use other sentences too, to get the same effect, but this provides a quick, easy and (for most) amusing way of introducing the subject of tonic stress.

Lesson 3: Misunderstanding dialogues: Contrastive stress (All levels)

Lesson type: Practice
Materials: Scripted dialogues

In this activity, a dialogue is used which involves a series of misunderstandings. The dialogue itself may seem rather artificial, but the exercise helps underline the idea of contrastive stress, and how moving a tonic syllable can change the emphasis of what the speaker is saying.

The teacher gives student B some lines to say, and student A is given a line which they will need to say in various ways, depending on what the misunderstood point is. The activity works better if there is no preparation, and students are put on the spot; they may not always get the point straight away, but it's worth persevering.

Student A	Student B
I'd like a big, red cotton shirt.	Here you are. A big, red cotton skirt.
No, I said a big, red cotton shirt.	Here you are. A big, red nylon shirt.
No, I said a big, red cotton shirt.	Here you are. A big, blue cotton shirt.
No, I said a big, red cotton shirt.	Sorry, I haven't got one.

To make the task slightly easier, the relevant stresses can be indicated on the students' role cards. A similar exercise is seen below:

Student A	Student B
It's a pity you weren't at the party.	I <u>WAS</u> at the party.
Did you say you were at the barbecue?	I was at the <u>PAR</u>ty.
Did you say Enrico was at the party?	<u>I</u> was at the party.

This kind of exercise can also be used to highlight strong and weak forms of function words, as we can see with *was*, in the example above.

Lesson 4: Listening and transcribing: Stress placement in a short monologue (All levels)

Lesson type: Practice
Materials: A tape recorded monologue (the recording is optional). Transcript of the monologue.

Listening exercises provide a useful opportunity for sentence stress recognition practice. The teacher plays or reads out the monologue. It is useful for students to hear the whole passage first, to get a feel for the content. The students are then given a transcript of the monologue, and mark stresses on their transcript when it is played or read again. The advantage of using a tape is that this ensures consistency when the monologue is played for a second time. The teacher makes sure that the second reading or playing includes suitable pauses to give students time to mark the stresses. Students then compare their transcripts and discuss them, before the teacher lets them hear the whole passage again. The class then goes through the transcript, with the teacher inviting students to mark the stresses on a 'master' version on the board or overhead projector, discussing where they go and why, and comparing sentences discussed with the version on the tape (if used). A final hearing of the passage gives a chance for students to confirm the results of their discussions.

An interesting variation of the activity is for students to record themselves talking; this can be either natural, unrehearsed and unscripted speech, or a more prepared piece, depending what you and your students have decided to focus on. Students can then mark stresses for each other on transcripts of the tape. Students can do this in pairs or groups (depending on the resources you have available), or the whole class can work on one transcript. It is important, however, not to single one student out as an example of a speaker using inappropriate or inaccurate stress; the activity is best done in the spirit of comparing and contrasting, particularly if the unusual stresses used, while different from those of a native speaker, do not seriously affect intelligibility. A student's tape can also be contrasted with a version recorded by the teacher. Recording does not necessarily need lots of 'out of class' preparation time; it can very usefully be incorporated into a lesson, either as a 'one-off', or as a regular activity.

This idea can of course be used for other aspects of pronunciation (such as spotting weak forms, and incidences of /ə/). Taping can also be particularly useful for working on tonic syllables and aspects of intonation. A transcript could have gaps where all the tonic syllables should be, for students to complete while they listen to the text. Or students (using an agreed and easy to use method of transcription) can mark where the tonic syllables occur on a complete transcript.

This type of activity can be graded according to the students' level of proficiency, and it is possible to successfully use variations of it with students ranging from elementary to advanced levels.

Lesson 5: Categorisation: Word stress (Elementary to Intermediate)

Lesson type: Practice
Materials: Task sheet

This type of activity requires students to categorise words according to their stress pattern. The words in this example exercise are all names of jobs and professions, and the activity might be used in a lesson working on language connected with this area. Teachers should, of course, try to tailor the activity to suit the needs of their students and the language or subject focus of particular lessons.

The teacher starts by eliciting one or two of the words which appear on the task sheet before handing it out. She also asks students to work with a neighbour to decide which syllables in the two words are stressed, and then elicits the answers. The aim here is just to make sure that students understand the subsequent task. Students, singly or in pairs, are then given a task sheet like the following:

Put these words into the correct columns, according to the stress pattern.				
Oo	Ooo	oOo	Oooo	ooOo
Plumber Electrician Doctor Journalist Musician Shop assistant Teacher Soldier Novelist Architect Carpenter Actor Policeman Fireman Lecturer Florist Businessman Artist Farmer Scientist Researcher Gardener Designer				

Activities like this can also be used for focusing on particular sounds. For example, to work on /ə/ with a class, the above activity might be followed up by asking students to look at the words again, to then try saying them (or listening to them on a tape), and underlining or otherwise marking all the incidences of the sound /ə/.

Categorisation can also help to highlight language tendencies, which students can apply to new words they come across. For example, students can be asked to categorise words which can have two grammatical forms (e.g. noun and verb), which we looked at on page 69. The teacher might simply read out these words, or they can be recorded on a tape. If you wish to use grammatical clues to help students categorise, then the words can be used in sentences, or better still in a continuous passage, as long as it doesn't sound too contrived. An example activity might look like this:

Listen to the tape. You will hear each of these words once. Put it into the correct column, according to the stress pattern you hear.	
import rebel increase export decrease insult content	
Oo	oO

One can, of course, vary categorisation activities in order to provide a different classroom dynamic; students might be given a word on a card, and asked to organise themselves into groups according to the stress patterns of the words they have, or to attach their cards to the board in columns.

Further ideas for activities

Reading aloud

This certainly has its place when it comes to working on any aspect of pronunciation, and is particularly useful for working on stress (and intonation). It can be used in combination with taping, as explained above, and can obviously be used to deal with pronunciation alongside the study of particular lexis and areas of grammar.

Whatever is being read out, students should be encouraged to pay attention to the ways in which stress (and intonation) affect the message overall, and how variations in stress can change, or indeed confuse, the meaning of utterances.

There are two main difficulties with reading aloud, however. Firstly, reading aloud can be stilted and unnatural, particularly if a learner is having problems recognising words within the text. This will have obvious effects upon stresses within the utterances. The second difficulty is slightly more theoretical, but relevant nonetheless: there are important differences between spoken and written language, and this may be a problem in that the teacher might be asking students to speak sentences which were not designed to be read out. Written sentences are often longer than spoken ones and more grammatically complex, giving students unnecessary problems with identifying stress and tonic syllable placement. Conversely, the teacher might mistakenly try to gloss over the differences, leaving students with a false impression of the spoken language.

Clearly the teacher needs to choose the text very carefully, and, if the above factors are allowed for, reading aloud can still be a very useful classroom activity. A text needs to be long enough to make the 'public' reading of it worthwhile, but not so long or complex that the task becomes daunting. Teachers also need to provide enough opportunity for rehearsal, focusing on the relevant pronunciation features. It is important to keep in mind that the task should be achievable, and that the aim is to give students a chance to perform the reading successfully and meaningfully; they should be able to benefit from and enjoy the reading.

If possible, texts should be chosen which can be divided up so that all the students can have a go at reading. One text divided up among (for example) sixteen students might not give each participant a big enough section to read out. Instead, a small selection of similar texts might be used, so that groups of students can rehearse them before the reading. It is clearly useful if students can read texts that they have written themselves and humour is always helpful, though it is important to be aware of the risk of using culturally bound or obscure jokes which students simply won't 'get'.

Examples of the types of text which might be used include:

- short biographies of well-known people
- texts about students' own countries or home towns
- accounts of places that students have visited
- short 'sketches' or dramatic pieces (see below for more ideas on using these)
- poetry

The latter can be particularly useful for dealing with stressed syllables and weak forms; most poetry is written to be read, and writers often have in mind how the piece will sound when read out loud. Well-known poems can be used (bear in mind cultural differences here – things that teachers are familiar with may not be so well-known to their students), and students can of course write their own.

Limericks are often used in class for working on rhyming words, and their comparatively strict structure also lends itself well to the study of stress placement. Inappropriate stress placement will generally be very obvious. Many limericks are designed to be bawdy, or to have double meanings, and teachers clearly need to choose carefully, with a view to what is suitable for their classes. With preparation, and examples to demonstrate how limericks work, students can successfully produce their own. The following was written by a group of Upper Intermediate students:

There was a young man from Spain
Who travelled abroad on a plane
He studied some grammar
And how to say 'hammer'
And then he went home on a train.

My own personal favourites are ones which play with language, or which deliberately 'break the rules' of limerick rhymes and patterns, but can be used to good effect nonetheless:

There was a young teacher called Wood
Whose students just wouldn't use 'could'
But a teacher called Woodward
Discovered they could could
And did so whenever they should.

A mathematician called Hyde
Proclaiming his knowledge with pride
Said 'The answer, my friend,

As you'll find in the end
Is that the square on the hypotenuse of a right-angled triangle is equal to
the sum of the squares on the other two sides.'

Haiku also provide opportunities for working on stress placement, with their rigid structure of three lines, the first and last having five syllables, and the middle one seven. In response to this haiku, prepared for a class to introduce the idea:

Words briskly flowing
Down the rivers of the mind
Gathering in pools.

an Intermediate group produced the following:

Students are talking
At the entrance of the school
Gathering in groups.

The examples produced are unlikely to win any literary prizes (though creative tasks can often reveal a wealth of hidden talent). But they usefully focus students' attention on the structure of a genre (a type of text), and how stress placement can affect the overall success of a piece. Useful work on weak forms can also be done, focusing on how successfully they fit around the stressed syllables, and how they contribute to the overall 'feel' of the text.

Drama, and acting out rehearsed scenes

Drama provides a perfect opportunity for working on language generally, and pronunciation in particular. Careful study of the script (if one is used) is necessary before performance of it, and in particular, the ways in which stress placement contributes to the meaning of the lines. Clearly it makes sense to combine this with the study of particular grammatical structures and lexical areas. Short scenes can be devised to work on recent areas of study. I have used 'waiter' jokes to good effect in this way, with Elementary level students taking on the roles of waiter, customers and restaurant chefs. An example script was as follows:

Customer: Waiter, what's this fly doing in my soup?
Waiter: It's doing the breaststroke, madam.

This was used to provide a reminder of a particular use of the present continuous, as well as the pronunciation of *doing*, and the placing of tonic syllables. The next example was used to practise the pronunciation of *Would you like ...?* (Both of these scenes were used in the same lesson, along with a few others at the end of a short course, as a way of revising some of the language points covered.)

Customer: Waiter, I'd like to see the manager.
Waiter: Certainly, sir. Would you like to borrow my glasses?

Scenes from well-known plays or films, scenes written by your students, scenes provided by yourself: all of these can be used to great effect, with enough time for practice and confidence-building before public 'performance'. I know one enterprising teacher who successfully coached a group of willing students through a pantomime performance of *Cinderella* as a pre-Christmas entertainment for the other students in the school.

Improvisation can be equally rewarding as a classroom activity, though obviously the lack of rehearsal is likely to show in the quality of the language during performance. If you have access to facilities for videotaping, or at least recording sound, reviewing improvisations can be an entertaining and revealing way of providing correction and discovering areas of language to work on in class.

Some teachers resist using drama in the classroom, and the best advice would be to use it if you feel confident in doing so. If the answer is affirmative, also bear in mind that many students balk at the idea of performing publicly (whether for personal or for cultural reasons) and the teacher should consider these factors carefully. You should also not expect your students to do anything in class that you yourself would not be prepared to do, so be ready to set an example and participate enthusiastically.

Putting sentence stress into perspective

Sentence stress is an integral feature of language which provides listeners with vital clues as to the salient points of the speaker's message. Other features are the grammar of the utterance, the lexical content, the particular phonemes which make up the utterance, and the intonation contour used to deliver the message. Although identifying stressed syllables is not something that is uppermost in our minds when speaking or listening, it is something which we are extremely sensitive to at an unconscious level. We are aware of how variations in stress affect the message being put across, but we seldom need to declare what we mean, or elucidate and elaborate on how our stresses have contributed to communication.

When it comes to deciding how to deal with particular utterances or particular types of utterance in the classroom, then planning is essential. If you have fully planned your lesson, then you will have accounted for all the different elements. If you have 'delivered' your lesson fully, then students will have been, in some way, exposed to all of the elements of the particular language item you are dealing with. Or, if you are concentrating on the phenomenon of stress itself, then you should ensure that you have chosen appropriate examples of the aspect of stress which you are hoping to practise with your students, and that your examples are suitably contextualised.

Whether you are dealing with stress as an aspect of particular language structures, or dealing with stress for its own sake, you should aim to ensure that your students have the opportunity to both distinguish it through receptive exercises, and to practise it productively.

Conclusions

In this chapter we have:
- considered the nature of stress and unstress, and thought about different levels of stress.
- considered both word stress and sentence stress, and thought about rules or descriptions of these aspects of language.

- considered the role that stress plays in highlighting significant information within sentences and utterances.
- discussed stress timing and syllable timing. It was concluded that English is neither exclusively stress-timed nor syllable-timed, but has a tendency towards the former.
- introduced tonic syllables and onset syllables.
- thought about how to integrate stress into teaching, and how to raise students' awareness of the role it plays.
- looked at some activities for focusing on both word and sentence stress.

Looking ahead

- In Chapters 6 and 7 we will look more closely at intonation and other features of connected speech, and see how we can integrate stress with these aspects.

6 Intonation

What is intonation, and why teach it?

The term **intonation** refers to the way the voice goes up and down in pitch when we are speaking. It is a fundamental part of the way we express our own thoughts and it enables us to understand those of others. It is an aspect of language that we are very sensitive to, but mostly at an unconscious level. We perceive intonation, understand it and use it without having to examine the intricacies of everything we say or hear.

In dealing with intonation in the language classroom, we need to examine the nature of these unconscious processes, bring them to the surface and show how we believe they work. To be of use to students, work on intonation in the classroom needs to focus on practice rather than theory. We need to show learners how the choices they make with regard to intonation serve to determine the meaning of utterances. Traditionally, theorists have attempted to show links between grammatical constructions and certain patterns of intonation. Although these theories are not 100 per cent watertight, they give us some useful and teachable rules of thumb for helping students to use intonation successfully.

As well as helping to determine meaning, intonation gives us clues about the attitude of the speaker, or how he feels about what he is saying. When listening to people speaking, we get clear messages about their attitude from the ways things are said. We can get a good idea, for example, as to whether someone is interested, bored, being kind, being honest or lying, and so on.

Such ideas can be used in the classroom to help underline the function of particular phrases and utterances.

Although certain aspects of intonation may be common to many languages, some of the ways in which intonation is used may be specific to particular ones. Scandinavian languages, for example, tend to pronounce unstressed syllables on a higher pitch than stressed ones, whereas we usually do the reverse in English. Italian tends to change the order of words in a sentence to stress a particular word where we would do this through intonation. Spanish intonation tends to have a noticeably narrower range than English. Speakers of these languages will almost inevitably carry their habits of intonation over into spoken English. There are languages in which intonation has quite a specific meaning function, such as the various Chinese languages. These are called **tone languages** and they use the voice in quite a different way. The pitch and movement of the voice on a syllable determines the meaning. An often quoted example from Cantonese is *ma*, which can mean *mother*, *hemp* or *scold*, depending on whether the voice goes up or down or stays level.

Students' difficulties with intonation are not helped by the fact that concentration on grammar and vocabulary often takes their attention away from this feature. Struggling to find the right words will mean that the smooth movement of intonation will be interrupted.

In short, intonation needs to be a feature of classroom language analysis and practice. This will help students towards greater expressiveness and articulacy in English, and also help them to a better understanding of some of the subtleties of native-speaker speech.

The main difficulty for teachers and students with regard to intonation is that its links with specific grammatical constructions or attitudes can only be loosely defined. The reason for analysing these links is that the same words and structures can be given different meanings, or convey a different attitude by altering the intonation. Grammatical and attitudinal analyses of intonation can offer no hard and fast rules, but they can help steer students towards appropriate choices of intonation.

More recent theories, particularly those developed by David Brazil, analyse how intonation relates to the surrounding discourse, rather than specifically to grammar or attitude. The term **discourse** defines any meaningful stretch of language. Analysing intonation within discourse means that the wider context of a conversation, or monologue, is taken into account, and enables us to see how intonation conveys ideas and information. Intonation helps us to indicate what is shared knowledge between the speaker and the listener and what is new information. In this approach, intonation patterns are no longer isolated and tied to particular grammar constructions or attitudes, but are related to the context in which they occur. The advantage of this approach is that it is possible to give clear rules with regard to the appropriate choice of intonation patterns in a given context.

In this chapter, we will look at approaches based on grammar, attitude and discourse, and consider examples of lessons which might be appropriate for each. Before we do that, however, we need to look in a little more depth at the workings of intonation.

Tones, tonic syllables and tone units

Utterances are made up of syllables and the syllables where the main pitch movement in the utterance occurs are called **tonic syllables**. The syllables that establish a pitch that stays constant up to the tonic syllable are called **onset syllables**. Thus, in the following example *lives* is the onset syllable, which is conventionally shown in capitals. *Lon* is the tonic syllable, which is conventionally shown in capitals and underlined.

she LIVES in LONdon

As we have done in this book up to now, we can also represent the intonation patterns in this utterance with an arrow:

She lives in London.

Notice that in this particular example the voice starts at a certain pitch, then goes up very slightly on the onset syllable and then stays level until the tonic syllable where the pitch falls noticeably. The pitch at which a speaker begins an utterance will depend on their own pronunciation habits, but will generally be higher than their normal habit if they are nervous or excited and lower if they are bored or very relaxed. The pitch that is held from the onset syllable to the tonic syllable is known as the **key**.

In the above example there is only one tonic syllable and we can say that the utterance is therefore composed of one **tone unit**. Tone units are conventionally noted by being enclosed within two pairs of slanted lines. So an utterance consisting of one tone unit is shown like this:

//she LIVES in LONdon//

An utterance with two tonic syllables and therefore two tone units can be shown as:

She's lived in London since she was twenty.

or, as:

//she's LIVED in LONdon// SINCE she was TWENty//

Note that the tonic syllable is the last stressed syllable in a tone unit.

As we indicated earlier in this chapter, a key feature of intonation is that we, as speakers, can use it to indicate to our listeners what we think is new information in a conversation and what is old, or already shared, information. Consider the following sentences where the intonation pattern is marked, as we have done up to now, with an arrow:

What time does your train leave?

What time does your train leave?

The first example shows a question asking for new information. The second version shows a question asking for confirmation of something the speaker thinks he has already been told. The words are the same, yet the intonation patterns used show a contrast between the two versions. As we can see the main movement of pitch is on the tonic syllable (in these examples, the syllable *train*). The main movements of pitch, within a tone unit, are called **tones**. In the first of the two questions above, the tone is described as a **fall**, and in the second as a **fall-rise**. These are shown in a commonly used notation system as ↘ and ↗. In this system the arrows are placed at the beginning of the tone unit, but refer to the movement of pitch on or around the tonic syllable (the underlined syllable). It has to be said, however, that the movements of pitch (the tones) are not always tied precisely to the tonic syllable, they can start before and can finish after the tonic syllable.

Employing this system of notation the various utterances used in this section can be expressed as follows:

(60)
// ↘ she LIVES in LONdon//
// ↘ she's LIVED in LONdon// ↘ SINCE she was TWENty//
// ↘ WHAT time does your TRAIN leave//
// ↗ WHAT time does your TRAIN leave//

In the classroom, for example when writing on the board explaining an intonation pattern of an utterance to students, teachers might find it more straightforward to use continuous arrows, such as those on page 88, drawn above conventionally written sentences. This approach enables teachers and students to concentrate their attention on the main pitch movements (the tones) within an utterance. The more complex notation system above can be a useful tool for teachers analysing intonation patterns particularly when they are planning lessons.

Grammar and intonation

Many attempts have been made to show connections between intonation patterns and particular types of grammatical structure, and the following list shows some of these. The reader will find it easy to say these examples in other ways; it should be remembered that these are generalisations rather than rules. They can, however, help in giving students guidance in making appropriate choices with regard to intonation:

(61) • **Information questions** with *Who, what , where*, etc: Falling intonation (if being asked for the first time), e.g. *What's your name? What's the time? Where do you live?*

(62) • **Questions** expecting a 'yes/no' answer: Rising (*Is it the blue one? Have you got a pen?*)

(63) • **Statements**: Falling (*He lives in the house on the corner. It's over there.*)

(64) • **Imperatives**: Falling (*Sit down. Put it on the table.*)

(65) • **Question tags** expecting confirmation: Falling (*You're French, aren't you? He's very tall, isn't he?*)

(66) • **Question tags** showing less certainty: Rising (*You're French, aren't you? Your train leaves at six, doesn't it?*)

(67) • **Lists** of items: Rising, rising and finally falling (*You need a pen, a pencil and some paper. The stall sells ribbon, beads, elastic and buttons.*)

As we have already seen with the example in the previous section, the same thing can be said in different ways. The question *What time does your train leave?* was used with both a fall, and a fall-rise, for different purposes. There is also more flexibility when it comes to 'yes/no' questions. We can and do sometimes use a falling intonation, for example when eliminating possibilities:

(68) Is it the blue one? ... No? Is it the red one, then? ... OK, is it the green one?

It is clear that the list above doesn't adequately cover the range of possible intonation choices available to speakers. However, it is also true that the teacher who applies these rules to their treatment of intonation in the classroom is unlikely to lead students astray; that is to say that in using these patterns, students will not go drastically wrong. The rules may not cover the full range of possibilities, but neither do they create problems. To make an analogy, a driving instructor cannot hope to teach all driving manoeuvres that exist to a student, yet those they do teach will enable the student to cope on the road and give them the confidence to discover more as they gain experience. Likewise, in teaching grammar we do not teach students everything there is to know about the present perfect the first time it is introduced. We give some basic rules with the aim of showing students how it can be used in certain situations. If they apply these rules students will not go wrong, but neither will they have covered the full range of possibilities.

The following sample lessons show some different ways in which the links between intonation and grammar can be practically used in the classroom. In line with the classification of lesson types described on page 14, the examples show intonation issues being Integrated with the teaching of a language point, being dealt with Remedially and being Practised in their own right. They also cover a range of different levels.

Lesson 1: Question tags (Elementary)

Lesson type: Integrated
Materials: Taped listening exercise, questionnaire, role cards

The teacher introduces the theme of nationalities, and checks that students can relate the names of countries to their adjectives (*England – English*, *China – Chinese*, etc). These can be drilled briefly to give students confidence in saying them. In a multilingual class, the students' own nationalities can be used; in a monolingual class, the teacher can 'assign' nationalities to students for the purposes of the lesson. The teacher elicits the idea of question tags by asking a Japanese student *You're Japanese, aren't you?*, with a falling intonation on the question tag. The same question can then be asked to students of other nationalities to reinforce the intonation pattern. Students, prompted by the teacher, can then ask and answer the question appropriately to each other across the class, and then ask their neighbours. The teacher can correct as necessary.

At this point the teacher can clarify the grammar of question tags by writing on the board:

You're Japanese, aren't you?

and pointing out that a positive statement is usually accompanied by a negative tag. A negative statement would normally be accompanied by a positive tag. The verb *to be* in the statement is repeated in the tag.

Next, in order to focus on intonation, the teacher can ask the question again, and ask the students whether his voice goes up or down on the tag. The downward movement can be practised with a further quick choral drill, and drawn on the board over the original example sentence.

The teacher then checks that the students have grasped the concept by asking them whether he is sure what the answer will be when he asks the question. It should be apparent that he is, from the practice that the students have done so far.

The teacher then asks the question with a rising intonation, saying it a couple of times in order to let the students hear the difference. He then asks the students if they can hear any difference, eliciting from them the fact that his intonation rises. The sentence can be drilled chorally and individually with the new pattern. The teacher then asks the question 'Am I sure?', eliciting from the students the idea that this rising pattern indicates less certainty on the part of the speaker. This can then be noted on the board next to or underneath the previous example.

By way of a further check, a listening exercise might then be used in order to give the students practice in discriminating between the two patterns. After setting the context (in this case a conversation in a student coffee bar) the following dialogue might be played:

(69)

A: Hello, my name's Koyomi.
B: Hi there, I'm Sara.
A: Hello Sara, nice to meet you!
B: Excuse me, Koyomi, you're Japanese, ↘aren't you.
A: Yes, that's right. I'm from Saitama.
B: I thought so. Your name sounds Japanese.
A: And Sara, you're Italian, ↗aren't you?
B: Yes, that's right, I'm from Torino, in the north-west.
A: I see. I thought you were either Italian or Spanish.
    Would you like a coffee ... (fade)

While listening to the tape, the students answer the following questionnaire:

> 1 Koyomi is from Japan: true/false
> 2 Sara is from Spain: true/false
> 3 Sara is sure that Koyomi is from Japan: true/false
> 4 Koyomi is sure that Sara is from Italy: true/false

Students can compare their answers when they have finished, and the tape can be played again if necessary, before the teacher gets feedback from the whole class. In this example, the correct answers are: 1 true, 2 false, 3 true, 4 false.

After the listening exercise, it is important that the students get some practice in using the new patterns. If the class do not know each other very well, they can find out each other's nationalities using the rising or falling question tags as necessary. They can use what they have learnt to engage in genuine communication. If the class <u>do</u> know each other they could do the following activity.

In this activity, students are assigned various nationalities. Each student in the class will need a role card. Here are two example cards:

You are Spanish.
You are sure that:
Two students are Japanese, one student is Brazilian and one is English.
You think that:
One student is Polish, two students are French and one is Chinese.

You are Chinese.
You are sure that:
Two students are French, one student is Polish and one is English.
You think that:
One student is Japanese, two students are Brazilian and one is Spanish.

While doing the activity, the students make a note of the nationalities they discover through doing the activity. Their task is to find all the nationalities present in the classroom. The activity leads them into using rising and falling question tags according to how sure they are. In either case, they may have their beliefs confirmed or contradicted.

The same lesson might also be done with the focus on another area, such as jobs, names or positions within a company. Subsequent lessons could investigate further the grammar of question tags, in that auxiliary and modal verbs used in the original statement will be repeated in the tag, and other verbs will be replaced by the appropriate form of *do* in the tag.

Lesson 2: Asking permission (Intermediate)

Lesson type: Remedial

In this lesson the teacher is dealing with some functional language for asking permission, such as:

Do you mind if I	*open the window?*
Is it alright if I	*turn the heating on?*
Could I possibly	*borrow your newspaper?*

In the lesson so far the language has been contextualised, elicited, drilled and concept-checked. The class is engaged in a role-play situation in which there is a need for the language to be used (for example, a student staying in homestay accommodation talking to the host family, or another context similarly relevant to their needs outside the classroom). While monitoring the activity, the teacher becomes aware that some of the students are using an intonation pattern that does not sound very natural. Some, for example, are treating the verb in each sentence as the tonic syllable, for example:

(70)   // ↘do you MIND if i TURN the heating on//

Other possible variations which might sound inappropriate are:

// ↘do you MIND// ↘if i turn the heating ON//
// ↘could i POSSibly// ↘BORRow// ↘your newsPAper//

The teacher decides that problems the students have with their intonation need some attention in order to help them complete their task effectively. Dealing with intonation at this point reinforces its role as a part of successful communication.

To do this, once the activity is completed, the teacher elicits the sentences again, one by one, and drills them chorally and individually. She then writes the sentences on the board and asks the students to tell her, for each sentence, where the voice goes down and up. If the students are not sure, the teacher can say the sentences aloud herself, to make things clearer. Once the answer has been elicited, the teacher draws arrows on the board to show the appropriate patterns:

Do you mind if I turn the heating on?

Is it alright if I turn the heating on?

Could I possibly borrow your newspaper?

Students can then copy the sentences with the appropriate intonation pattern into their notebooks for reference when studying. The previous activity might then be tried again, with the intonation patterns fresh in the students' minds, or the teacher can move on to any subsequent activities she had planned.

Lesson 3: Instructions and questions (All levels)

Lesson type: Practice
Materials: Tape of two native speakers, typed transcript, worksheets

This activity involves listening closely to native-speaker communication in order to concentrate on intonation patterns, and then imitating them. The patterns are then related to grammatical areas. The lesson involves some preparation, but the resources may be used again with different classes.

The teacher needs to have a tape of two native speakers talking in an unrehearsed and unscripted way. The easiest way is to record yourself and a friend having a chat. (It is always important to get the permission of anyone whose voice you wish to record before using it in the classroom.) The recording needs to be very clear, and ideally the speakers should not talk over each other too much. If possible, the tape should include a variety of statements, questions, question tags, etc. A useful situation to record would be that in which one person is instructing another, who might be engaged in something like cooking, where statements, questions and instructions are likely to be used. The tape should be about 2–4 minutes long. This should provide enough language for useful study. The teacher will also need to type out the transcript of the tape and worksheets as necessary. The following activities are just suggestions; bear in mind that the activities will ultimately depend on the content of the tape, and the particular needs of the classes you use it with. The same tape might also be used with different level classes, using different tasks.

In class, the teacher can pre-teach any necessary vocabulary for the tape, and also do some work in order to set the context. This is important, as the context could be seen to have an influence on the language and intonation patterns used. The best way to establish the context is to let students listen to the tape for the first time while doing a written task with questions like *Where are they?* and *What are they doing?*, which will help them get a general idea of what the tape is about. Other possibilities depend obviously on the content of the tape, but questions like *Do they agree?* or *Which person is better at cooking?*, for example, can link in nicely with the intonation study that follows. This type of activity can help prevent misunderstanding and disagreement, and help focus the students directly on the important information.

If the teacher feels that these open-ended questions might not work with a particular class, he can focus on the same ideas by setting a multiple-choice task, or an exercise requiring a 'true/false' type answer, such as the following:

1 Bill and Jane are	in the kitchen at an office in the garden
2 They are	cooking a meal trying to get a machine to work
3 Who is better at it?	Bill Jane
4 Bill makes some mistakes	true/false

After letting students compare their answers and getting feedback from the whole class, the tape can be played again to ensure all the students understand the key points of the listening passage. This time, the students will have a transcript of the conversation, but with the words which contain the tonic syllables blanked out. Depending on the class, the teacher will either pre-teach the relevant words, or assume that the class will not have too much difficulty with them. While listening, students fill these words in the blanks. The teacher can pause the tape from time to time in order to give the students time to write the words down.

After checking the answers, the teacher tells the students to mark intonation patterns on the tonic syllables. The instruction can be general (i.e. to mark all rises and falls), or selective (e.g. just falls, or just fall-rises), depending on the students' knowledge of intonation, and the aspects that the teacher wishes to focus on. Even if the students have spent a lot of time working on intonation, it is always worthwhile demonstrating the activity by doing the first one or two examples with the whole class, to ensure that all of the students know exactly what their task is.

At this point, students can have their first attempt at imitating the voices on the tape. Having divided the text into manageable units the teacher plays the tape, section by section, with students repeating after each section. Students can imitate one or both speakers (depending on what the teacher wants to focus on, the quality of the tape, and how much or how little the people speak over each other). Students can repeat chorally, and the teacher can randomly nominate individuals for each line, eliciting any corrections as necessary. The advantage of imitation at this stage is that students' minds are focused only on the intonation patterns.

Once the intonation patterns have been practised, the teacher can ask students to mark on the transcript which of the utterances are statements, which are questions, which are question tags and so on, according to the focus of the lesson. These can then be compared with the intonation patterns already highlighted and practised. Students (depending on their abilities) might simply be asked to describe the intonation patterns, if the teacher feels this is an achievable task. If not, a worksheet might be given in order to narrow down the range of possible answers. Such a worksheet might look something like this:

Match these intonation patterns to the sentence types		
Sentence type	Examples	Intonation pattern
Question Statements Lists	A: How much do I put <u>IN</u>? B: You put it in the <u>BOWL</u>. C: You need <u>FLOUR</u>, <u>MILK</u> and <u>BU</u>tter.	1: ↗ ↗ ↘ 2: ∨↗ 3: ↘
Question tags	D: It shouldn't look like <u>THAT</u>, should it?	4: ∨↗

(The correct answers to this exercise are: A 2/4, B 3, C 1, D 2/4.)

The class can then go back to the tape and do more practice based around this, or they could apply their new knowledge to a different situation, such as being asked to demonstrate or discuss particular skills with a partner. It is very useful if the students can do real demonstrations at this point. Things like making paper aeroplanes, or doing origami, or drawing cartoons can easily be set up in the classroom, and offer a good opportunity to practise giving instructions and asking questions. If these demonstrations can be taped, the teacher then has further material to use for the analysis of intonation (and perhaps for comparison with the original tape).

Attitude and intonation

Another way of looking at intonation is to consider how it varies according to the speaker's attitude towards a situation. For example, the simple sentence *That would be nice* (in response to an invitation, let's say) might show enormous enthusiasm, mild pleasure, surprise, relief, sarcasm and boredom, amongst other possibilities. In real face-to-face communication many things contribute to how the message is delivered and understood including, for example, our observation of the speaker's body language, and our knowledge of his personality and likes and dislikes. Intonation gives important indications, but it is also important to appreciate that our choice of grammar and vocabulary can also be a very obvious indicator of our attitude towards a situation!

The main difficulty in trying to make a link between intonation and attitude in the classroom is that the same intonation pattern can be used to express wildly differing attitudes. When we are speaking in a matter-of-fact way we usually use a succession of falling tones (for example, // ↘ *its over* *THERE*// ↘ *on the TAble* // ↘ *next to the NEWSpaper* //). However we could describe the intonation of someone who is expressing a sense of relief in the same way. There are other differences here, such as the starting and finishing pitch of the speaker's voice and the length of the vowel sounds, but the basic intonation pattern is the same.

However, teachers can do some useful work with relating intonation to attitude in the classroom in the same way as we did with grammar and intonation. In dealing with the links between intonation and attitude, the classroom setting allows us the opportunity to work on the confident use of intonation. We can tie intonation work in with teaching and practising particular set phrases, and also work on the range of intonation (how high or low the voice goes) which students feel comfortable using when speaking English; classroom work on intonation sometimes requires students to use patterns which feel alien to them, and they can feel embarrassed about repeating patterns, or be reluctant to use the range the teacher models for them. Also, concentration on grammar and lexis can mean that the range students use is narrower than it might otherwise be.

The following sample lessons show some different ways in which the links between intonation and attitude can be practically used in the classroom.

The first of these deals with the intonation we use with **lexical phrases**. Lexical phrases are phrases which we use in ordinary, everyday communication, but which have the characteristic that they lose their meaning if broken down and analysed. They may be seen to occupy the middle ground between vocabulary and grammar. Some examples are as follows:

How do you do?
How are you?
See you later.
See you soon.
At last!
Look on the bright side.
Don't get me wrong…
As for me…

Such expressions are a major feature of our language. The degree to which they are idiomatic varies; that is to say, some may be seen as wholly idiomatic, like *It's all water under the bridge*, whereas others can be more literally analysed for meaning, like *See you later*. Other phrases may be considered as 'sentence builders', in that they are not complete in themselves; an example of this is *As for me...* .

An interesting feature of lexical phrases from the point of view of intonation is that many such expressions are delivered as tone units, having one main tone movement. For example, on being introduced to someone for the first time, in a relatively formal setting, the following would be an appropriate utterance:

(73) // ↘HOW do you <u>DO</u>//

This is a complete expression, and the falling intonation is itself a part of the message.

The expression *Don't get me wrong...*, which might be used when giving a personal opinion, can often have the following pattern:

(74) // ↗DONT get me <u>WRONG</u>//

The expression will clearly be followed by other information, but is characteristically delivered with a predictable pattern, as shown.

Other expressions may not constitute a complete tone unit (remember that this is an utterance or part of an utterance with one main tone movement) but may be used to introduce one. For example, *I'm not sure whether to...* is often used to introduce a couple of possible choices for a particular action. The phrase is not a tone unit in itself, but can have a relatively level intonation, before the main choices, carrying the tone movements, are introduced:

(75) // ↗im NOT sure whether to go to <u>SPAIN</u>// ↘or <u>POR</u>tugal//

A similar introductory expression is *What do you make of...?* which can be used to elicit a viewpoint from the listener. It is often used with a relatively level intonation pattern, prior to the main information in the utterance:

(76) // ↘WHAT do you make of that new <u>TEA</u>cher//

In the following activity, the fixed expressions used are practised with appropriate intonation patterns, as ways of presenting one's views in a discussion.

Lesson 4: Expressing views (Intermediate+)

Lesson type: Practice
Materials: Video/audio tape of television/radio discussion (optional), two worksheets

The teacher chooses, or asks her students to choose, a topic for discussion, perhaps an issue such as the importance of recycling waste, something in the news, or something relevant to the students' current situation, like the food available in a school's coffee bar or the provision of self-study materials. At the beginning of the lesson, the teacher canvasses the range of opinions in the classroom, not worrying too much at this stage about the language students use to express themselves. The views can be summarised on the board, using columns to represent opposing views.

The teacher then asks the students to brainstorm different ways of arguing a point, using the opportunity to elicit or give appropriate phrases. Alternatively, a video or audio recording of a discussion from a television or radio current-affairs programme might be used, if available. The following are some suggestions of phrases you might like to use. Onset syllables, tonic syllables and intonation are indicated:

// ⟋DONT get me <u>WRONG</u>//
// ⟍i COULDnt agree <u>MORE</u>//
// ⟋AS for <u>ME</u>//
/WHAT do you make of...
// ⟍i DONT think you can <u>SAY</u> that//
// ⟍THATS not the <u>POINT</u>//

As these are elicited the teacher takes the opportunity to drill them chorally and individually; this is important, as the way the expressions sound will give important clues as to the attitude of the speaker to the discussion. Then students are given the task of listening out for stressed syllables and for intonation patterns. The expressions can be given on a worksheet, and the teacher can say the expressions out loud. The teacher and students should agree on a method of marking intonation. It is important to use the same methods regularly, so that students become familiar with them. The students are then asked to match the utterances with the appropriate attitude, as shown in the following worksheet. If the teacher has been working from a video or audio tape, this can be used again at this point to help the students. If not, the teacher can model them again.

Underline the stressed syllables and mark the intonation patterns:	Match the phrases on the left with these ideas:
As for me...	I'm going to say something you might not like.
I couldn't agree more.	I'm showing strong disagreement.
Don't get me wrong, but...	I'm about to give my point of view.
What do you make of...	I disagree.
I don't think you can say that.	I'm showing strong agreement.
That's not the point.	I'm looking for your opinion.

The students have now had the phrases introduced to them, have practised saying them with appropriate intonation patterns, and have done an exercise to show how the words and intonation combine in terms of the speaker's attitude to the subject matter and to the discussion in general. They are now ready to have a go at using them productively themselves. The teacher can now return the students' attention to the subject introduced at the start of the lesson, and set up a discussion based around the topic. The students now have the opportunity to try using the phrases and accompanying intonation patterns in an appropriate setting. If possible the students' debate should be recorded for later analysis, as this provides a valuable opportunity for further study.

Lesson 5: Expressing attitudes (Elementary+)

Type: Practice and Remedial
Materials: Cards with imaginary presents written on, prompt cards with adjectives written on, role cards

Close attention to grammar and vocabulary when practising language can mean that intonation suffers. Students' speech may well sound less natural, and the flow may be interrupted, as students search for the right word or construction. This activity gets students working with easy sentences, relieving them of the need to concentrate on grammar or vocabulary and enabling them to concentrate on intonation. A further purpose of this activity is to help students explore the ways in which they use their voice range (how high or low their voice goes) when speaking English, and to introduce various ideas which may subsequently be used remedially, as reminders. Activities like this can help give students greater confidence in their intonation use.

The teacher writes *mmm* on the board, and asks students to think about the different ways they can say it. He elicits a couple of examples (e.g. // ↘*mmm*// and // ↘↗*mmm*//) and then gives students a short time to brainstorm other examples. He then elicits these from the students and writes them onto the board, suggesting if necessary, until the following variations are there:

// ↘mmm//
// ↘↗mmm//
// ↗mmm//
// ↗↘mmm//
// →mmm//

The teacher then asks students to think about what these mean. The first one // ↘*mmm*// could indicate *I agree*. // ↘↗ *mmm*// indicates *I agree, but...* //↗ *mmm*// tells us that the speaker wants the listener to say more. // ↗↘*mmm*// might indicate strong agreement, and //→*mmm*// could reflect boredom or lack of interest. The teacher then asks the students to substitute the word *yes* for *mmm*, and drills the patterns before letting the students experiment with them. The implied meanings are the same.

Each pattern is then drilled again, but exaggerated somewhat; a falling pattern starts higher and ends lower, and a rising pattern starts lower and ends higher. The teacher then asks the students if exaggerating the range affects the meaning; the idea here is to establish that the bigger range indicates a greater degree of emotion.

The teacher writes *thank you* on the board. He gives out present cards to the students. Some of these are quite exciting gifts, like a new Ferrari, or £10,000. Others are quite the opposite, like a tin of peas, or a toilet brush. The students then give presents to their neighbour, saying *Thank you* to each other in accordance with how they feel about their present. The range used should reflect how excited (or not) students are by their presents.

This can be followed up by working on other simple sentences. It is important to choose sentences appropriate to the students' level. These could be sentences which use a structure which the students have recently studied, and which are ambiguous enough to be used in a variety of situations, or flexible enough to be said in a variety of ways, reflecting different attitudes. Examples might be sentences like *I'm meeting her at nine*, *I saw him yesterday*, or *I think that's mine*. It makes sense to avoid sentences in which the words used are themselves direct indicators of attitude (e.g. *I don't like this food*), as different ranges of intonation wouldn't be so appropriate. The example used is *Good morning, Mr Johnson*.

With the whole class, the teacher elicits which syllables within the sentence are stressed. It is important that these remain constant, otherwise the activity will become an exercise in how changing stress affects meaning, which is not the aim here. The teacher asks students to work in pairs or small groups in order to brainstorm, and to practise saying the sentence in a variety of ways. These are then tried out and discussed with the whole class. The teacher uses this opportunity to introduce a set of prompts, which can be written on cards and held up as necessary. Examples might be: *neutral, happy, bored, sympathetic, excited, surprised, friendly, unfriendly, businesslike*, and so on. The teacher drills the sentence according to each prompt card, and students repeat in chorus, and individually. The class can then discuss the range of voice used, which will be wider the more 'extreme' the attitude held, or emotion felt. It is important to bear in mind throughout that the teacher is not teaching the students anything they do not do in their own language, though English does, as mentioned earlier in the chapter, use a wider range of intonation than many other languages. This activity aims to allow students to forget about grammar and vocabulary, and concentrate on different ranges of intonation, gaining confidence in using them.

Students are subsequently given a selection of role cards, outlining their previous relations with Mr Johnson. For example:

1   You've never met Mr Johnson before. You want to do business with him.
2   Mr Johnson owes you a lot of money.
3   You think Mr Johnson is a pleasant man.
4   You're secretly in love with Mr Johnson. (optional)
5   Mr Johnson is wearing women's shoes.
6   You really don't like Mr Johnson.

Students then work in groups, with one playing Mr Johnson, and the others greeting him appropriately. 'Mr Johnson' has to try to work out (roughly, not exactly) the attitudes towards him, from the various ways in which he is greeted. There will clearly be other clues here, such as facial expression and body language, but Mr Johnson can usually get a fair idea from the intonation used.

The prompts introduced earlier in the activity can be kept and used as reminders in subsequent lessons, or, if practical, put up on the wall of the classroom.

Discourse and intonation

A discourse approach to intonation examines how the stresses we make, and the tone we employ when speaking, relate our utterances to the surrounding language. The term 'discourse', as mentioned at the start of the chapter (page 87), refers to a stretch of meaningful language. Intonation can be used to present ideas and information within utterances, conversations or monologues. A simple example is seen in the idea of listing. If we say *You need a pen, a pencil, and some paper* the voice tends to rise on *pen* and *pencil*, indicating that there is something more to come. The voice may then fall on *paper*, to indicate that that is the end of the list.

(67)

The wider context of conversations is important, and we can see how the speaker's intonation indicates his interpretation of what is shared knowledge and what isn't. In the sentence:

(77) When you get to the office, you'll see a tall man named Sean.

the name *Sean* is a new piece of information, and the voice falls on this word. A following sentence shows a different effect:

(78) When you see Sean, give him this letter.

This time, there is a fall-rise on *Sean*, indicating that the name is now shared knowledge. It also helps indicate that the rest of the instruction is to follow. The choices we make, while being for the most part unconscious, help us to guide and control our conversations. The advantage of this approach over the grammatical/attitudinal indicator approaches is that clear rules can be given with regard to appropriate choices of patterns.

The most basic intonation choice is between what are known as **referring tones (r)** and **proclaiming tones (p)**. The two most frequently used tones in English are the **fall** and the **fall-rise**. A falling tone is called a **proclaiming tone (p)**, and the fall-rise is a **referring tone (r)**. (These terms and ideas were originally developed by David Brazil.)

We can think of the choice between these tones as indicating two alternatives. One alternative is that the speaker is expressing information that is presumed to be new, or is adding something to the discussion. In this case a proclaiming tone is used. We also use the proclaiming tone to give facts, express opinions we believe to be true, or to ask for new information. The other alternative is that the speaker is referring to information that he presumes to be shared between the speakers. In this case a referring tone is used. In questions, we use a referring tone to make sure what we are saying is correct, or to check information. Consider the examples on the next page:

(79)

Example	Explanation
//↘WHAT time does your <u>TRAIN</u> leave//	I'm asking you for a piece of new information. A **p** tone indicates this.
//↗WHAT time does your <u>TRAIN</u> leave//	You've told me the train time earlier, but I have forgotten. I use the **r** tone to indicate that there has been shared information, and to make sure.
//↘she's LIVED in <u>LON</u>don// //↘since she was <u>TWEN</u>ty//	I'm telling you some facts about her that you don't know. The **p** tone indicates that this is new information.
//↘he LIVES in the house on the <u>COR</u>ner//	I'm telling you a fact about him that you don't know. The **p** tone indicates that this is new information.

Taking the last two examples from the previous table, let's see how a change in tone might reflect the utterances being used in different situations, where there is some shared knowledge:

(80)

Example	Explanation
//↗she's LIVED in <u>LON</u>don// //↘since she was <u>TWEN</u>ty//	We both know that she lives in London; the shared information is shown by the **r** tone in the first tone unit. You have asked me how long she's lived there. This new information is reflected by the **p** tone in the second tone unit.
//↘he <u>LIVES</u> in the house on the corner//	We both know that we're talking about the house on the corner. You have just said *John's buying the house on the corner, isn't he?*. I'm telling you something you appear not to know, and this is shown by the **p** tone on 'lives'.

As we saw on page 88, the onset syllable usually sets a pitch which carries on until the tonic syllable is reached. This constant pitch is called the **key**. Using a high key usually means that the speaker is contrasting something with what has been said before. Starting a conversation with a high key is usually a good way of engaging the interest of the listener. A mid-key usually adds something to what has been said, and a low key indicates that the information is a natural follow-on from before. The key is of course relative, in two ways: it is relative to what has been said before, and also relative to the speaker's voice qualities and typical speaking habits.

The following sample lessons show some different ways in which the relationships between discourse and intonation can be highlighted and practised in the classroom. The examples show intonation teaching being Integrated with the teaching of a language point, being dealt with Remedially, and being Practised in its own right. They also cover a range of different levels.

Lesson 6: Making deductions (Intermediate to Advanced)

Type: Integrated

In this lesson, students are given a puzzle to solve, and the language they need in order to discuss the possible answers to the puzzle is taught and practised. To start, the teacher sets the context and pre-teaches any vocabulary she feels might be necessary. Any activities which require the students to discuss an issue, put forward suggestions and draw conclusions might be used (for example, trying to interpret ambiguous photographs or drawings). In this example the students have to decide how events have led up to a given outcome.

The teacher sets up the first situation:

> A man with a pack on his back entered a field, and died.

The students are given some time in small groups to discuss possible answers, but the teacher does not give one at this point. After students have had the chance to discuss, the teacher asks them to note down the language they used while deciding on their answers. The teacher writes any suitable suggestions on the board, and takes the opportunity to elicit or to give the following language.

> He might have been attacked by an animal.
> He could have been attacked by an animal.
> Perhaps he was attacked by an animal.
> If he was attacked by an animal, he could have run away...
> He can't have been attacked by an animal. That's too easy.

The students will be clear about the concepts involved in this kind of language as they will have produced it themselves, prompted by the situation itself and with the teacher's assistance. To make sure, however, the teacher asks questions like 'Do we know if this happened?' and 'How sure are we?' First, just one suggestion is worked with, so that the students see the intonation patterns emerging.

The sentences are then drilled, and the students are asked to write the utterances down, and mark the stressed syllables and tone movements. Students can underline stressed syllables, and draw arrows to show tone movements; remember it is important to use notation systems consistently with your students, so that they become familiar with them. The following uses the notation introduced in this chapter:

(81) // ∨he <u>MIGHT</u> have been// ↘aTTACKED by an ANimal//
// ∨he <u>COULD</u> have been// ↘aTTACKED by an ANimal//

// ⍔ perHAPS he was// ⍓ aTTACKED by an ANimal//
// ⍔ if he WAS attacked by an animal// ⍓ he COULD have run aWAY//
// ⍓ he CANT have been attacked by an animal// ⍓ THATS too EAsy//

Consistencies in the intonation patterns can be shown by applying them to another example:

(82)

// ⍔ he MIGHT have been// ⍓ PArachuting//
// ⍔ he COULD have been// ⍓ PArachuting//
// ⍔ perHAPS he was// ⍓ PArachuting//
// ⍔ if he WAS parachuting// ⍓ he COULD have used a resERVE//
// ⍓ he CANT have been parachuting// ⍓ THATS too EAsy//

These too can be drilled chorally and individually, and the consistencies highlighted on the board. Students can do further practice by supplying their own mysteries to be solved.

Lesson 7: Indirect questions (Pre-Intermediate to Intermediate)

Type: Remedial

A lesson is in progress, and the students are working on an activity involving indirect questions. They are doing a speaking activity where the language being practised is as follows, within the context of seeking information from a stranger:

	the bank	
	the post office	
Do you know where	the chemist's	is please?
Could you tell me where	the doctor's	
	the bus station	
	the police station	

While monitoring, the teacher notices that some students are using a falling tone on the verbs, and using two tone units, as in:

// ⍓ do you KNOW// ⍓ where the BANK is please//
// ⍓ could you TELL me// ⍓ where the BANK is please//

A more appropriate way of asking these questions, given the context, would be:

(83)

// ⍔ do you KNOW where the BANK is please//
// ⍔ could you TELL me where the BANK is please//

Here there is one tone unit, with the main tone movement (a fall-rise) being on the noun. The verbs are stressed, and set the key. The teacher writes the nouns on the board (if they are not already written there), and re-eliciting the question forms (*Do you know where...* and *Could you tell me where...*), he drills them chorally, using a high, but level key. He then drills the end of the sentences, using the fall-rise appropriately, on and after the nouns. He then points to each alternative noun in turn, and either repeats a choral drill, or asks individuals to say the sentences. He then completes the question forms on the board, and draws arrows, as shown below. Tonic syllables are underlined, and in capitals.

Do you know where	the BANK is please?
Could you tell me where	the POST office is please?
	the CHEMist's is please?
	the DOCtor's is please?
	the BUS station is please?
	the poLICE station is please?

The pattern here is quite clear. While this is not to say that the sentences must be or will always be said in this way, the suggested intonation is at least appropriate. By pointing out such consistencies the teacher will help students both to recognise them and be more likely to remember and use them. The teacher can then either ask students to repeat the activity, or move on to other practice activities, as he feels is necessary.

Lesson 8: Tone units (Advanced)

Type: Practice
Materials/Resources: Tape recorder, video camera and player, transcript of student's presentation

A teacher is working one-to-one with a student who needs to give a presentation at a conference. In rehearsing the presentation, the teacher notices that the intonation and tone units used by the student affect the quality of the presentation.

In this kind of situation, if the resources are available, the teacher could either tape-record, or better still video the student giving a trial run of the talk. Using a transcript of the talk, the teacher takes the student through some examples of tone units used, helping her to listen out for the falls and rises made. On a fresh transcript, the teacher helps the student to re-group the tone units, drilling and practising as necessary. Another recording can be made when the student feels confident enough to try the whole thing again; this recording can be listened to and compared with the original.

How teachable is intonation? The fact that the same thing may be said in different ways, at different times and for different reasons, leads to a potentially bewildering range of choices for students. A part of the art of successful teaching is in helping students to narrow down the number of available options, and to make appropriate choices with the language they use. This should also be the teacher's aim when teaching intonation. We saw in Chapters 3 and 4 how phonemes contrast with each other, so that in particular circumstances a sound constitutes an appropriate choice (as seen in minimal pairs, like *hit* and *heat*). Likewise, as we saw in Chapter 5, we can label syllables within utterances as stressed or unstressed, and depending on the circumstances, stressing or not stressing a syllable will be appropriate. If we treat classroom intonation in the same way, we have a system that is workable for students; we can demonstrate which intonation patterns are appropriate for a given situation. Investigating the links between intonation and certain types of sentence, and intonation and attitude, can be helpful to a degree. However, the analysis of intonation in spoken discourse gives a relatively straightforward way of describing and narrowing down a whole range of intonation possibilities. By concentrating on tonic syllables, and by showing an initial choice between referring and proclaiming tones, we divide those possibilities into two groups which can then be analysed further. Most students will not want or need a full analysis of proclaiming and referring tones; teachers can, however, help their students listen out for tonic syllables, and for whether the voice goes down or up, and so help them narrow down the choices. The significance of intonation is best dealt with in clear contexts, and through the analysis of examples, with ample opportunity for both receptive and productive work.

It has been claimed, by some, that intonation is unteachable and that it operates at such a deep level of consciousness that it can only be acquired through long-term exposure to a second language. Language teaching and learning are in part a process of bringing subconscious mechanisms to the surface, studying them, and pointing out patterns. A lot of our language may be considered automatic and the processes of production and interpretation operate at a subconscious level, particularly in ordinary, everyday speech. If we can analyse and show patterns in the grammatical and lexical properties of our language in the classroom, then why can't we do the same for intonation as well?

Many teachers would admit to finding it difficult to hear whether or not their own voice is going up or down. However, it is much easier to spot when a student is using the wrong kind of intonation in practice activities in the classroom. Many teachers already do remedial work on intonation in the classroom without necessarily realising it, through re-drilling sentences, getting students to say things again, and so on. It is really a question of taking time to listen out for intonation yourself, and of gaining an understanding of how it works. Work on intonation can, and should be, built into lessons from beginner level to advanced level.

Conclusions

In this chapter we have:
- described intonation as the changes of pitch our voices make when we are speaking.
- looked at intonation as being an aspect of language that we are usually only aware of at a subconscious level. We have also seen how intonation is used in different ways in different languages, and that it is therefore an important area of study for language

learners. Working on intonation in the classroom can help students towards a better understanding of English, as well as greater expressiveness and articulacy.

- considered three ways of approaching the study of intonation:
  - connecting intonation with grammar
  - connecting intonation with attitude
  - connecting intonation with the surrounding discourse
- looked at the link between intonation and sentence stress, and shown how spoken language can be divided into tone units, each tone unit having one major tone movement. In discourse analysis falling tones are known as proclaiming tones, and rising ones as referring tones. Analysis of intonation with reference to the surrounding discourse can help to illustrate how speakers indicate what is shared, and what is new information.
- seen that while intonation patterns can be linked to certain grammatical constructions, these are not invariable rules. However, we can still use them for valuable practice in the classroom. We have also drawn similar conclusions with regard to the connection between intonation and attitude. Intonation can, at times, help listeners to understand the attitude of speakers to what they are saying. Again, while this may only provide us with a rough guide, useful work can be done with students in this area.
- shown how consistency is important in teaching intonation. We do not need to show students the full range of choices available in a particular situation, but, in applying consistent patterns we can help them to narrow down their options, and use the patterns they have learnt appropriately.
- argued, finally, that intonation is both learnable and teachable.

Looking ahead
- Chapters 5 and 6 have shown how stress and intonation help us to vary the message conveyed through connecting strings of phonemes. Chapter 7 looks at other aspects of connected speech, and in particular, at what happens when phonemes meet.

7 Other aspects of connected speech

- Why 'other' aspects of connected speech?
- Assimilation
- Elision
- Linking and intrusion
- Juncture
- Contractions
- Should we teach these aspects of connected speech?
- Sample lessons
    - Lesson 1: 'Getting to know you': Assimilation and weak forms
    - Lesson 2: 'Going to': Weak form
    - Lesson 3: Phrasal verbs: Linking
    - Lesson 4: Superlative adjectives: Elision
    - Lesson 5: Elision and other features of connected speech

Why 'other' aspects of connected speech?

In Chapters 3 and 4, we dealt with the individual sounds, or phonemes, which we use when speaking. Our aim in considering these phonemes was to investigate how they are articulated, so that we are better able to help students over difficulties with understanding and producing these sounds. The ultimate aim of this is, of course, to help students understand and produce not just individual sounds, but the strings of phonemes which make up utterances.

As we have seen in previous chapters, these longer utterances are subject to the influence of the stresses we make, and the tone movements we apply, according to the message we wish to convey. Word stress, sentence stress and intonation are aspects of connected speech, in that they apply (usually) to more than one phoneme. Weak forms, such as where *are* is pronounced as /ə/ in *Her eyes are* /ə/ *lovely*, are an aspect of connected speech too. (For a fuller explanation and a list of weak forms, see pages 73–75.) In this chapter we will look at further aspects of connected speech, in particular what happens when phonemes meet.

It is useful here to make a distinction between careful speech and rapid speech. The features we are looking at will usually be more evident in rapid, everyday speech. In more careful speech (such as when delivering a talk, for example, or when modifying our speech for social purposes such as teaching), we may tend to use them less. Certain features may also be more or less common in different accents and varieties of English, and personal habits and preferences also have an influence.

Assimilation

(84)

The term **assimilation** describes how sounds modify each other when they meet, usually across word boundaries, but within words too. If we consider the words *that* and *book*, and look at the phonemes involved, we get /ðæt/ and /bʊk/. If we then place the words into a sentence (for example, *Could you pass me that book, please?*), we notice that the /t/ phoneme at the end of *that* does not sound like it does in the word said on its own. The phoneme /t/ is an alveolar sound (see page 7 for the sound chart), which is formed when the tongue blade forms a temporary closure against the alveolar ridge. If you try saying the sentence a few times over, you will notice that the tongue doesn't actually get there at the end of the word. Rather than having our tongue make the unnecessarily long journey all the way to the alveolar ridge, we employ an economy of effort, and get our articulators (in this case the lips) ready for the next sound, /b/. The modified sound retains its original voice quality, and so we say that the /t/ assimilates to a /p/, both sounds being unvoiced. As a result, we get *Could you pass me* /ðæp bʊk/? This is not to say that we give the /p/ its full plosive manner of articulation either, as we would if we were to say the non-word /ðæp/ on its own, merely that our lips are in the position to make a /p/. The best description is that in readying our articulators for the next sound, certain sounds are either absorbed, or modified into others. There is another possibility: the /t/ at the end of *that* could also become a **glottal stop**, where the glottis (the opening between the vocal cords inside the larynx – see page 4) closes momentarily.

Other examples involving the same sounds as the above are:

(85)

Can you see tha<u>t b</u>oy over there?

Where has the ca<u>t b</u>een all night?

Who's a cu<u>te b</u>aby, then?

Some rules for assimilation

(86)

1 The phonemes /t/, /d/ and /n/ often become bilabial before bilabial consonants /p/, /b/ and /m/:
> He's a rather fa<u>t b</u>oy. (/t/ assimilates to /p/)
> She's got an apar<u>tm</u>ent in Manhattan. (/t/ assimilates to /p/)
> He's a very goo<u>d b</u>oy. (/d/ assimilates to /b/)
> There are te<u>n m</u>en in the class, and two women. (/n/ assimilates to /m/)

2 /t/ assimilates to /k/ before /k/ or /g/. /d/ assimilates to /g/ before /k/ or /g/:
> Where has tha<u>t c</u>at been all night? (/t/ assimilates to /k/)
> Can you see tha<u>t g</u>irl over there? (/t/ assimilates to /k/)
> It was a very goo<u>d c</u>oncert. (/d/ assimilates to /g/)
> She's a very goo<u>d g</u>irl. (/d/ assimilates to /g/)

3   /n/ can assimilate to /ŋ/ before /g/ or /k/:
I've been going out too much lately.
He's bringing his own car.

4   /s/ can assimilate to /ʃ/ before /ʃ/:
I really love this shiny one over here.

5   /z/ can assimilate to /ʒ/ before /ʃ/:
We found this lovely little cheese shop in Paris.

The above examples are cases of **anticipatory assimilation**, where one sound changes to another because of the sound which follows. Here are some cases of **coalescent assimilation**, where two sounds combine to form a different one:

6   /t/ and /j/ coalesce to form /tʃ/:
You went to France last year, didn't you?

7   /d/ and /j/ coalesce to form /dʒ/:
Would you like a cup of tea?

Elision   The term **elision** describes the disappearance of a sound. For example, in the utterance *He leaves next week* speakers would generally elide (leave out) the /t/ in *next* saying /neks wiːk/. Again here, the reason is an economy of effort, and in some instances the difficulty of putting certain consonant sounds together while maintaining a regular speech rhythm and speed.

Some rules for elision
(87)   1   The most common elisions in English are /t/ and /d/, when they appear within a consonant cluster.
We arrived the next day. (/t/ elided between /ks/ and /d/)
When we reached Paris, we stopped for lunch. (/t/ elided between /tʃ/ and /p/, and between /p/ and /f/)
We bought a lovely carved statuette. (/d/ elided between /v/ and /st/)

2   Complex consonant clusters are simplified.
She acts like she owns the place! (/ækts/ can be simplified to /æks/)
Teachers use authentic texts to teach from. (/teksts/ can be simplified to /teks/)
George the Sixth's throne (/sɪkθs θr/ simplified to (/sɪks θr/)

3   /ə/ can disappear in unstressed syllables.
I think we should call the police. (/ə/ can disappear in the first syllable of *police*)
I'll love you forever, promise. Well, perhaps. (/ə/ can disappear)
It's a question of collective responsibility. (/ə/ can disappear)
Are you coming out tonight? (/ə/ can disappear)
That's an interesting idea. (/ə/ is not pronounced by many speakers, reducing the number of syllables in the word)
Have we got any vegetables? (/ə/ is not pronounced by most speakers, reducing the number of syllables in the word)

4 /v/ can disappear in *of*, before consonants.

My birthday's on the 11th o**f** November.

It's a complete waste o**f** time!

That's the least o**f** my worries!

Linking and intrusion

When two vowel sounds meet, speakers often link them in various ways.

Linking /r/

Some accents of English are described as **rhotic** /ˈrəʊtɪk/, which means that when the letter *r* appears in the written word after a vowel (as in *car* or *carve*), the /r/ phoneme is used in the pronunciation of the word (as in /kɑːr/ and /kɑːrv/). Examples are most dialects of American English, Irish English and certain British regional accents. Other accents are **non-rhotic**, and do not pronounce the /r/, so we get /kɑː/ and /kɑːv/. RP (Received Pronunciation) is non-rhotic. When, however, there is a written *r* at the end of a word and it occurs between two vowel sounds, speakers with non-rhotic accents often use the phoneme /r/ to link the preceding vowel to a following one:

(88) He**r** English is excellent. (/r/ is pronounced)

He**r** German is absolutely awful, though! (/r/ is not pronounced)

My brothe**r** lives in London. (/r/ is not pronounced)

My brothe**r** always phones at the wrong time. (/r/ is pronounced)

Intrusive /r/

Where two vowel sounds meet and there is no written letter *r*, speakers with non-rhotic accents will still often introduce the /r/ phoneme in order to ease the transition. This happens when the first word ends in /ə/, /ɑː/ or /ɔː/. Speakers with rhotic accents tend not to do this:

(89) Princess Diana was a victim of medi**a e**xploitation. /əre/

The medi**a a**re to blame. /ərɑː/

It's a question of la**w a**nd order. /ɔːrən/

I sa**w i**t happen. /ɔːrɪ/

Some speakers also let an /r/ intrude within words like *drawing* (pronouncing it as /ˈdrɔːrɪŋ/) and *gnawing*.

Linking /j/

When a word ends in /iː/, or a diphthong which finishes with /ɪ/, speakers often introduce a /j/ to ease the transition to a following vowel sound:

(90) **I a**gree, wholeheartedly. /aɪjə/

I think, therefore **I a**m. (Descartes) /aɪjæm/

I am, therefore **I o**ught to be. (G. Kelly) /aɪjæm/ /aɪjɔːt/

The**y a**re, aren't they? (linking /j/, and linking /r/) /ðeɪjɑː rɑːnt/

This happens because in order to form /iː/ and /ɪ/, the mouth is in more or less the same position as it is for the start of the semi-vowel /j/.

Linking /w/

When a word ends in /uː/, or a diphthong which finishes with /ʊ/, speakers often introduce a /w/ to ease the transition to a following vowel sound:

(91)

Go on! Go in! /gəʊwɒn/ /gəʊwɪn/
Are you inside, or are you outside? /juːwɪn/ /juːwaʊt/
Who is? /huːwɪz/
You are. /juːwɑː/

This happens because in order to form /uː/ and /ʊ/, the mouth is in more or less the same position as it is for the start of the semi-vowel /w/.

Juncture

Try saying the sentence *I scream, you scream, we all scream for ice-cream*. Although the phonemes involved in the underlined words are the same, subtle differences help us tell the deed from the dessert. The same subtle differences in the use of phonemes are also found in the underlined words in the following two sentences:

The clock keeps ticking. /kiːps tɪkɪŋ/
The kids keep sticking things on the wall. /kiːp stɪkɪŋ/

The differences in the pronunciation of the underlined words, despite the fact that the phonemes are the same, are differences of **juncture**. A deeper analysis of such examples would show differences in the length of vowel sounds, variations in degrees of syllable stress, differently timed articulation of the consonant sounds and allophonic variations too. So, while the phonemes may be the same, listeners have no difficulty (most of the time) in telling where the join is, and context clearly plays a role here. Other examples showing the same phenomenon are:

(92)

That's my train.
It might rain.
The great apes
The grey tapes

In the pair

Can I have some more ice?
Can I have some more rice?

the linking /r/ could lead to confusion over juncture, but again context and subtle differences in articulation help us to judge which one we have heard. Students may not have the necessary background knowledge needed in order to make the distinction.

Consonants often seem to be attracted across word boundaries:

(93)

You'll need an egg, an olive and an anchovy. (... a negg, a nolive and a nanchovy)
Put it on. (pu ti ton)

The *negg*, *nolive* and *nanchovy* are obviously non-words, but occasionally the coincidence of sounds can lead to examples where listeners may hear an unintended word:

It's no joke. (snow)
It's tough. (stuff)

A famous example concerns a misheard lyric from the Jimi Hendrix song 'Purple Haze', where the line *'Scuse me, while I kiss the sky* was heard as *'Scuse me, while I kiss this guy.* Assimilation also plays a role here, in the assimilation of the /k/ in *sky* to a /g/.

Contractions

Contractions occur where two words combine to the extent that the two are pronounced as one word, or one syllable. These have (for the most part) become conventionalised in written language. Common examples are as follows:

I'm /aɪm/, you're, he's, she's, we're...
I'm not /aɪm nɒt/, you aren't, we aren't...
Can't /kɑːnt/, won't...
Would've /wʊdəv/, could've...
Couldn't /kʊdnt/, wouldn't...

There are restrictions, however. We can say *You're not* and *You aren't.* We can say *I'm not*, but *I amn't* is unusual, and seen as incorrect. Examples like *would've* and *could've* are often understood by children learning written English as being a contraction of *would of* and *could of*, (the weak form of *of* being the same as the weak (and contracted) form of *have*). For a significant number, this misinterpretation persists into adulthood and is such a common error that it is sometimes to be found on the lyric sheets of pop music CDs.

Should we teach these aspects of connected speech?

In the same way that working on sentence stress and intonation can help students to better understand spoken English, so can working on the other features of connected speech. In many cases, the simple awareness of their existence can help enormously in enabling students to better understand the language they hear. In so saying, the question for this section is answered. Or is it? There are two further questions that arise. Firstly, how far should we actively encourage and indeed train students to produce these features of connected speech, and secondly, should we give the different features equal weight in our teaching?

Over recent years there have been significantly different views expressed on whether to attempt to teach a productive ability in areas such as assimilation and elision. Some take the view that these areas should not be taught because to expect their successful production in students' speech is asking too much. Other commentators take the view that simply exposing students to the features of connected speech is enough in itself since students will then naturally and without prompting incorporate them into their own speech. If the latter view is true then it will be more likely to occur when the same features occur in the students' L1 (as can be the case with certain types of assimilation, for example).

Others also say these features should be ignored because if students do not produce them, this will not have a damaging effect on the intelligibility of what they say, or because such features will sound out of place in speech that is not entirely fluent. A further reason that has been expressed is that students see such forms as not 'correct' and will be unwilling to overcome their reluctance to use them as a result. Indeed some commentators take the view that a student is right to be reluctant as they see these features of connected English speech as simply signs of laziness and lack of education, and feel that they should be discouraged among native speakers, let alone being taught to students.

The reverse set of views is that these features of connected speech should be taught to students and encouraged in their production, particularly in the case of young children, who tend to be excellent mimics of new language, and better able to adopt unfamiliar pronunciation patterns. Others assert that adult students should be trained in a productive capacity in these features of connected speech, since not to do so will leave students sounding overly formal and somewhat stilted in their speech.

Overall the most common feeling seems to be that some of the features of connected speech are worth working on for productive use and others rather less so. It is possible to gauge which features are generally considered more worthy of attention, and which less, from a review of what items generally receive attention in coursebooks (and supplementary materials), and which do not.

- Contractions (and to some degree, weak forms) are often addressed in published materials; these features seem to be readily accepted as standard teaching points, and useful aspects of language to focus on.
- Linking sounds and intrusive sounds are also focused on in materials but to a lesser degree than contractions.
- Assimilation is also dealt with, but usually only in relation to very specific examples like *don't you?* and *didn't you?* both with a resulting /tʃ/.
- Elision is also taught in coursebooks, but again largely through very specific examples like *Do you live in London?*, and *Where do you live?*, both with a resulting /dʒ/. Other examples of elision (and indeed assimilation) are not so easy to find.

Contractions are probably given the greatest amount of attention of all the features of connected speech because they are represented differently in writing from full forms (*aren't* versus *are not*, for example). Since contractions are easy to represent in a written form, and as students will have to develop a written competence in them, they might as well develop a spoken one as well.

The other features of connected speech have no conventionally written form, so what other measure can we use to decide their value to students as productive tools? The degree to which they contribute to 'intelligibility' is a possible measure of their value. However, it is true to say that students who do not use these features but whose English is otherwise clear and correct are likely to be perfectly intelligible. An alternative measure is the issue of 'naturalness' of speech. It seems to be the case that native speakers tend not to notice features of connected speech when they are used, but do notice when they are not. Speech without the use of contractions can sound rather over formal in certain situations and indeed at times unfriendly. Certain features have become standardised within words so that it sounds odd if an established assimilation and elision is not used: for example, people who pronounce *sandwich* as /'sændwitʃ/ are in the minority, and the absence of any /t/ in words like *cas<u>t</u>le* and *whis<u>t</u>le* is expected. With regard to word boundaries, on the other hand, we are unlikely to consider the full realisation of /d/ in *goo<u>d c</u>oncert* as 'wrong', for example, just as we are unlikely to pay much attention to its assimilation to /ɡ/.

Yet another measure of the value of teaching a productive capacity in the features of connected speech is that of 'teachability'. There are two sides to how teachable an item is; on the one hand there is the likelihood of students being able to perceive the sound contrasts highlighted and put into practice the teaching they receive, and on the other there is the question of how confident the teacher is about being able to explain the issue under study, and deal with unexpected problems that may crop up. A painstaking presentation of *would've, could've, should've* and so on can often be followed by students doggedly sticking to the uncontracted forms in a subsequent practice activity. However, the same can be said for grammar and vocabulary presentations, to a lesser or greater degree. This should not be taken, therefore, as a reflection of the teacher's or students' abilities, but as an inevitability in the process of learning a language. Students will only begin to use new language and new features of language successfully and consistently when these have become fully apparent and relevant to them. Contractions and weak forms, for example, should be considered teachable, but teaching something does not usually guarantee its immediate use. The key thing is that teachers need to be confident in their understanding of the 'rules' of connected speech before attempting to study these with students. A confused explanation can be worse than no explanation at all. An informed teacher is more likely to be aware of the features discussed, and more likely to be aware of when they might be important, and therefore more likely to be able to teach them effectively.

Finally, there is the measure of 'relevance'. Is a productive capacity in the finesse of connected speech relevant to the students' needs and personal pronunciation targets? These are determined usually by the environment in which the students use their English outside the classroom. A student who lives and/or works in a relatively informal English-speaking environment is more likely to come across these features, and to benefit from working on them both receptively and productively. A further aspect to relevance is how relevant the features of connected speech are to the particular language item being dealt with in the lesson. This is important when it comes to thinking about the full integration of pronunciation into language teaching.

Ultimately, every teacher has to make their own judgements, based on the above criteria, of how much attention to give to the various features of connected speech. But to return in a way to the original point in this section, attempting to teach a productive competence in connected speech, however successful this turns out to be, is a very good way of enhancing students' understanding of fast and fluent connected speech.

Sample lessons

Below are some examples of how features of connected speech can be worked on in the classroom for both receptive and productive purposes. The examples show certain features being Integrated with the teaching of a language point, being dealt with Remedially, and being Practised in their own right. They also cover a range of different levels.

Lesson 1: 'Getting to know you': Assimilation and weak forms (Beginner to Elementary)

Lesson type: Integrated

Here the teacher utilises the real context of the classroom with a new class, who don't know each other very well. The main aim of the lesson is to teach or revise some basic 'personal information' questions. As part of the language work, the pronunciation of these questions is also being taught. The activity can also be used perfectly adequately with a class who do know each other, but are using role-play for the purposes of practising the language. The lesson focuses on various examples of assimilation and the weak forms which can be used in these questions. Some teachers may feel uncomfortable teaching these pronunciations at such an early stage, and it has been argued that one should teach 'proper' forms before teaching assimilations, elisions and weak forms. However, if pronunciation is to be properly integrated into language teaching, then it's best to start right at the beginning. Remember that students may well be asked the questions they are studying with this 'natural' pronunciation outside the classroom (depending on their circumstances, of course), even if only when signing up for their course.

The teacher writes a large question mark on the board, along with the following words:

> Name:
> Live:
> Job:
> Age:

The teacher then points to the word *name*, points to the question mark, gestures to the class, and says 'Ask me a question'. She elicits the question *What is your name?*, and uses her fingers to help students appreciate that there are four words. Pointing to each finger in turn she asks the class to provide the words, not worrying about pronunciation particularly at this stage. Once the class is clear that there are four words, the teacher puts the first two fingers together to elicit *What's*, as opposed to *What is*. This can be briefly drilled on its own, though only with the aim of helping students to see that these two words are being contracted. The teacher then points to the *your* finger, and says 'pronunciation?', eliciting suggestions. The teacher then drills the weak form /jə/ chorally and individually. Then putting the first three fingers together, the teacher similarly elicits and drills /ˈwɒts jə/ (some might also pronounce this as /ˈwɒt ʃə/) chorally and individually. Finally, the teacher uses the last finger to elicit *name*, before drilling the whole sentence. The teacher asks the question to two or three students, before using 'open pairs' (see page 17) across the classroom, with students asking and answering. Students then briefly ask and answer the question with their immediate neighbours (depending on the layout of the class).

The same procedure is gone through for the other questions, with the pronunciations to be worked on listed below:

Live: /weə dʒə lɪv/
Job: /wɒt dʒə duː/
Age: /haʊ əʊld əjuː/

Students are then given a handout with a table on, on which they can record the personal information of other students, as they mingle and ask questions. The teacher can include more information, or adapt the questions as she feels is appropriate for the class. As part of a written record of the language, the teacher can write on the board phonemic symbols to indicate the assimilations and weak forms dealt with for the students to copy down. If the students are not familiar with the symbols, this can act as an introduction to them.

Lesson 2: 'Going to': Weak form (Elementary to Pre-Intermediate)

Lesson type: Remedial

The teacher has been practising *going to* with a class, using a context of talking about plans for a holiday or trip. The students have been working in groups, planning an itinerary for a trip to the UK, and then in new groups each student has outlined their plans to their fellow students. While monitoring this activity, the teacher notices a range of different pronunciations of *going to*. This had not been worked on at the start of the lesson.

Some students are using the weak form of *to* (/ˈgəʊɪŋ tə/) before both consonant and vowel sounds (/ˈgəʊɪŋ tuː/ would be more appropriate before a vowel sound, the two being linked by a /w/), some are using /ˈgəʊɪŋ tuː/ before both vowels and consonants, but without the linking /w/ and some are using /ˈgɒnə/ or /ˈgʌnə/, which they have picked up from somewhere.

At the end of the activity, the teacher elicits some of the itinerary ideas from the students, writing on the board examples like the following:

```
visit London
eat fish 'n' chips
go to Brighton
```

The teacher also writes *going to* on the board, and asks the students how it is pronounced, accepting the suggestions from the class with no correction at this stage. He then points to the first verb (*visit*), and asks again how *going to* is pronounced. He listens for /ˈgəʊɪŋ tə/, and takes the opportunity to drill it both chorally and individually. Underneath the word *to*, he writes /tə/. He then elicits the pronunciation of *to* before *eat*, drills, and writes /tuː/ on the board, and writes up a /w/ on the board, to indicate the linking sound. He then elicits the /tə/ pronunciation before *go*, and points out that this is the same as the pronunciation before *visit*.

He elicits the reasons for these pronunciations, and makes a note to do some more work on this in future lessons. Here again, while using alternative pronunciations will probably not affect students' intelligibility, in drawing their attention to the existence of these features in the speech of many native speakers of English, the teacher is helping students to notice features which they may well come across later.

Lesson 3: Phrasal verbs: Linking (Intermediate)

Lesson type: Practice
Materials: A picture of a messy bedroom

The teacher wants to do some work with the class on the linking sounds /r/, /w/ and /j/. The class has recently been working on phrasal verbs, and the teacher decides to use these as a basis for pronunciation work. He initially uses a context of housework, and chooses a selection of phrasal verbs which are deliberately similar in meaning, so that work on the meaning of these is minimal and does not take time away from the main pronunciation focus of the lesson. The teacher shows a picture of a messy teenager's bedroom, and elicits the following verbs and sentences:

He's got to clear away the empty plates and cups.
He's got to clear out his cupboard.
He's got to clear up the mess.
He's got to tidy away his clothes.
He's got to throw out his old clothes.
He's got to throw away his football comics.
He's got to tidy up his desk.

As each sentence is elicited, the teacher drills it chorally and individually, then going on to drill each phrasal verb in turn. When this is done, he writes the verbs on the board, and shows the linking /r/ between *clear* and *away/out/up*, the /j/ between *tidy* and *away/out/up* and the /w/ between *throw* and *out/away*. The fact that some of these may be used interchangeably is dealt with if students ask, but otherwise the teacher keeps the focus on pronunciation. Students are then given a brief practice activity, in which they ask each other how often they themselves clear up, tidy up etc.

As can be seen from the above description, phrasal verbs offer a good opportunity for practising the linking sounds /r/ /w/ and /j/. They can also be used to show how a final consonant can move from the end of the previous word to attach itself to the beginning of the next word. In other words, the consonant may be 'attracted' across a word boundary as here:

get out (/t/ attracted to beginning of *out*)
walk out (/k/ attracted to beginning of *out*)
come out (/m/ attracted to beginning of *out*)

Lesson 4: Superlative adjectives: Elision (Pre-Intermediate to Intermediate)

Lesson type: Integrated
Materials: Pictures of tall buildings, or a relevant article from a magazine or from the *Guinness Book of Records*

The teacher shows or draws pictures of three buildings of different sizes. The class have recently worked on comparative adjectives, and so the teacher elicits the fact that building A (for example) is taller than B. She then elicits the fact that C is taller than A. She then gestures to indicate all three buildings together, and says *Tell me about C*. She elicits the word *tallest* /tɔːlɪst/. She drills the word to work on the sounds (particularly the /ɪ/ sound in the second syllable). She then drills the sentence *C is the tallest* (the buildings can of course be named, if pictures of real ones have been used), and writes the sentence up on the board.

The teacher then asks the question *Which is the tallest building in the world?*, and waits to see if anyone knows the answer (currently the Petronas Tower, Kuala Lumpur). If not, the answer is given. She writes:

> The Petronas Tower ... tallest building ...

on the board, and asks the class to give her a sentence, eliciting *The Petronas Tower is the tallest building in the world*. This sentence (replace the name of the building with *it*, if this is simpler) is then drilled.

Underneath the words *tallest building*, the teacher writes the phonemic script: /tɔːlɪs̲t bɪldɪŋ/.

She then points to the underlined /t/ phoneme, and asks the students to listen while she says the two words together a few times. She asks if they notice anything about the sound, and elicits the fact that the sound 'disappears', when the two words are said together. She drills the words a few times, and then drills the sentence again, chorally and individually.

She then introduces another idea, the world's biggest country, or fastest mammal, for example, eliciting and briefly practising a sentence to show the same elision of /t/. Ideally, students are then given access to reference material (for example, the *Guinness Book of Records*, or a relevant newspaper or magazine article), and asked to work in small teams to write questions for a quiz. If no reference material is available, students can use their general knowledge to perform the same task, or the teacher can provide them with the information they need.

Having written their questions, the teams take turns to ask them to the other teams; a point is awarded when a team gives a correct answer.

Competitive activities like this can often be rewarding and motivating as classroom activities, and this particular task gives the students the opportunity to practise the grammatical form of superlative adjectives as well as a feature of their pronunciation, when put together with a following noun. Of course, examples where the following noun begins with a vowel sound (e.g. *biggest animal*) will not show elision of /t/, but this can be used as a contrast in order to further underline just when the /t/ can disappear.

Lesson 5: Elision and other features of connected speech (Intermediate to Advanced)

Lesson type: Practice
Materials: Sound or video recording of natural speech

The teacher uses a cassette or video recording where one or two people are talking. The source of the recording is not very important; the teacher could even use a coursebook tape recording which has previously been used for another classroom purpose. However, the more relevant and interesting the tape is to the students, the more useful it will be in helping them to work on the features the teacher wants to investigate.

In the following example, the teacher is using a tape of himself talking about his family. He plays the tape, integrating its use with some comprehension questions or other tasks if it is appropriate to do so. The students having listened to the tape, the teacher briefly explains the pronunciation feature (in this case elision) and plays the tape again up to the first example which is *I live in South London, with my wife and* /ən/ *three children...*

He stops the tape at this point, and uses phonemic script on the board to help underline the point, showing the weak form of *and*, and how the /d/ has been lost, comparing it with how the word sounds when said with its 'full' pronunciation /ænd/. The teacher then asks the students to listen out for the next example of elision, and to shout out when they think they have spotted one.

When this happens, the teacher asks the student who has shouted out to explain the elision to the rest of the class (describing any related weak forms), coming to the board and writing it down using phonemic script if necessary. The students then briefly discuss whether or not they feel this is an appropriate example, with the teacher acting as adjudicator as necessary. The process can be repeated until the teacher is happy that students are confidently spotting examples of the feature.

Students are then given a transcript of the tape. This could be all in phonemic script if the students feel confident using it, or just written out alphabetically, whichever the teacher feels is more appropriate. In this lesson the students are given an alphabetic transcript, and are asked, while listening to the tape, to underline words or pairs of words together where they feel that they have spotted an example of elision. The tape is played in sections of about 10–15 words at a time (depending of course on the actual content, natural pauses between tone units provide the best opportunities to stop), giving students time in between to make their annotations to the transcript. The tape can be played as many times as the students seem to need, or as the teacher feels is still useful. It is important that the students are given time at the end to compare and discuss their answers with each other, and that the feedback from the exercise is thorough, with each example being dealt with, explained and practised as necessary. It is important that the tape is not too long, and that it includes clear examples of the features being worked on.

Practice lessons like this can be invaluable in helping students to decode rapid, connected speech. While we may not realistically expect all students to incorporate such features consistently into their own language, they are at least becoming aware of these features.

Following on from the previous activity, students can be asked to prepare a short talk on the same topic as the tape they have watched or listened to. Alternatively, students might choose to discuss an issue raised on the tape. Ideally, the students' presentations or discussions will be taped, and the resulting samples of spoken language can be analysed for the features being concentrated on.

If enough tapes are available, groups of students can work together to analyse samples, preparing an analysis, or giving each other advice with regard to the features being studied. The teacher will, at times, need to act as adjudicator, and perhaps also intervene to correct advice which doesn't quite work.

Conclusions

In this chapter we have looked at the technicalities of connected speech:

- assimilation, or the ways in which sounds can affect or modify each other when they meet.
- elision, or how phonemes can disappear.
- the ways in which adjacent sounds can be joined, and how other sounds are used to ease the movement from one sound to another.
- the junctures between sounds, and how there are subtle clues which help us to discern where one word ends and another begins.
- weak forms (which were first introduced in Chapter 6), and contractions.

We have thought about why it is useful for students to study these aspects of connected speech, and described how they can be studied and practised in class.

Looking ahead

Chapters 3 to 7 have examined the main features of English pronunciation, and suggested ways in which these can be meaningfully dealt with in the classroom. We now move on to examine the complex relationships between pronunciation and spelling.

8 Pronunciation and spelling

- **English spelling is not phonetic**
- **Regular features of English pronunciation and spelling**
- **Problems and approaches in the teaching of pronunciation and spelling**
- **Sample lessons**

  Lesson 1: Spelling of suffixes and the pronunciation of /ə/

  Lesson 2: Different spellings of vowel sounds

  Lesson 3: Wrong spelling test: Spelling/sound relationships

  Lesson 4: Dictionary work: Spelling/sound relationships

  Lesson 5: 'Trevor's Day': Present simple tense, final *s* as /s/ or /z/

English spelling is not phonetic

George Bernard Shaw, in a possibly idle moment, created the nonsense word *ghoti*, saying it should be pronounced in the same way as the word *fish* /fɪʃ/. He explained this by demonstrating how the pronunciation of *gh* could be taken from words like *tough* /tʌf/; the *o* could be taken from women /wɪmɪn/, and the *ti* could be taken from words like *notion* /nəʊʃən/. What he was showing was that there is not a one-to-one correspondence between spelling and pronunciation in English. The 44 different sounds we use when speaking English are written down using only 26 letters. This means that although there obviously is some correspondence between sounds and letters, many letters can represent more than one sound. This is seen, for example, in the letter *a*, which can represent /æ/ as in *apple*, or /ɑː/ as in *ask*, amongst numerous other possibilities. With consonants too, the letter *c* can be pronounced as /k/ as in *can*, or /s/ as in *cinema*. To add to the complication, many sounds can be represented by more than one letter or combination of letters; for example, /ʊ/ appears in <u>p</u><u>u</u>t, <u>book</u> and <u>could</u>.

In some languages there is a high level of correspondence between spelling and pronunciation; Japanese, Italian and Spanish are good examples of so-called 'phonetic' languages. Somebody learning Italian who is familiar with the sounds (or phonemes) represented by the individual letters, and by various combinations of letters, can, in theory, work out how a word they have only read should be pronounced.

Since the relationship between spelling and pronunciation is more complex in English, it is not always easy for learners of whatever L1 to see how a written English word should be pronounced, or how a word they have only heard should be written. But it is not the case that learners will always have to make a complete guess in such circumstances, nor that they will have to learn the spelling and pronunciation of thousands of words without recourse to any general rules. This is because English spelling is not as irregular as it seems. Surveys of the system have shown that over 80% of English words are spelled according to regular patterns, and that there are fewer than 500 words (out of an estimated total of over half a million words) whose spelling can be considered completely irregular. The fact that some of these words also happen to be amongst the most common ones (e.g. *are, said, come, how, what, could*) gives a distorted impression of irregularity in the system. Proficient readers, as well as applying sounds to individual letters, can also successfully recognise and apply sounds associated with groups of letters. For example, the pronunciation of *could* might seem quite irregular, but it can appear quite regular, following exactly the same pattern as *should* and *would*.

By tying spelling closely in with pronunciation work, teachers can show rules and patterns to students which they can then apply when they come across new words, be they heard or read. Regular features of English spelling and pronunciation can be shown to apply to individual letters of the alphabet and also across many different words.

Regular features of English pronunciation and spelling

Bringing the following general features of English to the notice of students may help them on many occasions. Being aware of the patterns and restrictions that exist in the system can make English less of an alphabet soup, and more of an organised yet flexible menu of possibilities.

Single letter and sound associations

In English there are 21 consonant letters, making 24 sounds, and 5 vowel letters, making 20 sounds. In the light of this, it is clear that vowels will be the most likely cause of pronunciation or spelling difficulties for learners of English. Many consonant letters have one main sound associated with them, such as *b, d, f, h, j*. Admittedly these letters can be silent in certain words, but this tends to only happen when they are immediately preceded or followed by another consonant in the same syllable; compare, for example, the silence of *n* in *autumn* and its pronunciation in *autumnal*. Letters that are related to a number of different sounds tend to have primary associations, and other less common ones. For example, *s* has the primary sound value of /s/ as in *gets*, but will have the secondary pronunciation of /z/ as in *has*. Similar observations can be made in relation to vowels. (For a more detailed analysis of these issues, see Appendix C on page 147.)

Letter combinations and sounds

Some pairs of letters are associated with a particular sound, as in the link between *ph* and the sound /f/, as in *photo, photograph* and *phone*. Such letter-pairs are known as **digraphs**. In certain cases, a digraph can have two or three different sound associations, depending on the words in question: *ch* for example, can be pronounced as /tʃ/ (*chip, change, hunch*), /k/ (*character,* *technique*) or /ʃ/ (*machine*). Note that there are rules in operation here; it is generally not possible, for example, for *ch* to have the sound /ʃ/ when it appears at the beginning or end of a word except in borrowed words like *charlatan, chignon* and *charabanc*.

With vowel digraphs, it is possible to identify primary and secondary values for particular pairings. For example, in the majority of words containing *ea*, the pair will be pronounced as /iː/ (as in *eat, heat* and *cheap*) which is therefore the primary value, while secondary values include the less frequent /eɪ/ (*great* and *break*) and /e/ (*dead, weather* and *breakfast*). (For more details on letter pairs and their sounds, see Appendix C and particularly Tables 4, 5 and 7.)

English letters behave according to their environment

Many English letters fit comfortably into certain environments, behaving in certain predictable ways when they are there. For example, many vowel letters, when sandwiched between consonant letters (as in *cap, cut* and *con*), will have the short vowel sound most commonly associated with that letter: /æ/, /ʌ/ and /ɒ/. The addition of a final letter *e*, will usually lead to a change to either a longer sound or a diphthong: *cape* /eɪ/, *cute* /uː/ and *cone* /əʊ/, making the written vowel 'say its name'. This also happens when other letters are added, as in *cuter* and *cones*. The *cute* example also shows us that with *u*, the addition of a final *e* often means that a /j/ is inserted before the vowel sound to make /kjuːt/; the same effect is seen in *tube* /tjuːb/ and *mute* /mjuːt/. The addition of a letter *r* immediately after the vowel letter will often lead to a longer sound: *carp* /kɑːp/, *curt* /kɜːt/ and *corn* /kɔːn/. (For more details, see Appendix C, Tables 6 and 8.)

Environmental restrictions

Sometimes the environments that single letters or paired letters can exist in are restricted. For example, *wh* usually appears at the beginning of words (as in *where* and *what*), sometimes appears in the middle of compound words (*nowhere* and *somewhere*), but doesn't appear at the end. Similarly, *ng* and *nk* appear at the end of words like *sing* and *sink*, in the middle of grammatical variations of those words (*singing, singer* and *sinking*), but don't appear at the beginning of words, except in names like *Nkomo* /ŋˈkɒmɒ/ and *Ng* /eŋ/.

Common patterns

In addition to the above, there are a number of common sound/spelling patterns which can be presented to students as safe and reliable. Here are some useful ones:

- When talking about the incidence of /ə/, it can be noted that /ə/ occurs only in unstressed syllables, and also in a high number of them. Spellings which students find difficult to pronounce can in fact be made much easier by concentration on this sound. It can be very useful to draw students' attention to its use in prefixes and suffixes, as these are usually unstressed: *technical, production, explanatory, bigger* etc.

- Common suffixes are usually consistent in their pronunciations, for example: *-tion* is pronounced /ʃən/ as in *explanation, pronunciation, promotion*; *-cial* is /ʃəl/ as in *special, official, prejudicial*; *-cious* is /ʃəs/ as in *precious, vicious, suspicious*.
- Certain vowels are usually elided in particular words: *secretary* /ˈsekrətriː/, *vegetable* /ˈvədʒtəbəl/.
- Certain spellings are usually assimilated in connected speech: *Would you, Could you*, using /dʒ/). This information can be helpful for lower level students, to help distinguish such words in listening comprehension activities.

'Root' words and derived words

It is frequently easy to spot related words in English, due to the fact that the spelling of the root word usually stays the same in the derived word. Often, the pronunciation stays the same too. For example, the root word *speak* /spiːk/ is unchanged in spelling and pronunciation in *speaks, speaker, speaking, loudspeaker* and so on.

Some words that have a common root, on the other hand, have drastically differing pronunciation; for example, the noun *sign* /saɪn/ has its own particular pronunciation, yet related words like *signal* and *signalman* follow the more phonetic /sɪg-/ pattern. However, simple patterns can still be shown; when *sign* is used as a verb, the related words *signature* and *signatory* follow the same pattern as *signal* and *signalman*.

At times, the stress in a word moves from one syllable to another when a different form of the word is used, and this can lead to a change in the pronunciation of a particular syllable. We can see this phenomenon in the words *invite* /ɪnˈvaɪt/ and *invitation* /ɪnvɪˈteɪʃən/, for example. However, it is clear that the words are related, and work can be done in class to show students how stressed syllables will tend to preserve their vowel sound, while unstressed ones will often change to a weak form.

An understanding of the regular features described above across a range of words can help students to predict the spelling of words they have only heard. The trained reader can also make very good guesses about the pronunciation of words which she has never encountered before, using her knowledge of how words typically behave. For example, the nonsense words *lum, lume* and *lurm* are completely predictable in their likely pronunciations.

Problems and approaches in the teaching of pronunciation and spelling

As we have said, the lack of a simple correspondence between the spelling system and the pronunciation system in English tends to cause problems for learners in that it can lead them to initially or repeatedly misspell words and mispronounce them.

The difficulties can be particularly acute for learners whose L1 has a more phonetic script system, like Japanese and Spanish and to a lesser degree French. Such learners may, for example, tend to try and give a sound value to every letter in an English word, leading to pronunciations like /wælked/ for *walked*. As a consequence they have to get to grips with a different way of thinking about the relationship between written and spoken language, such as the fact that /ə/ can be represented by a variety of spellings, or that *ough* has eight possible pronunciations (see page 7).

For all learners whose own language has an alphabetic script similar to that of English, a further problem can arise. Occasionally, a letter that is associated with a particular sound in L1 may be linked to a different sound in L2. In Spanish, for example, the letters *g* and *j* can represent a sound similar to the *ch* at the end of *Bach*. Spanish speakers may use this sound for an English *g* or *j*. In German, as another example, the written letter *w* is pronounced as /v/ (leading to pronunciations like /vaɪn/ for *wine*), and the letter *v* is pronounced as /f/ (leading to *very* being pronounced /feriː/).

Although spelling does appear to be a significant cause of pronunciation errors, not all of these are caused by the complexity of English spelling or by learners incorporating generalisations from the spelling/sound relationships of their L1 into their speech in L2. Spanish, for example, does not allow the sequence of *s* + another consonant at the start of a word without a preceding vowel; so, words like *stop* and *spell* may be pronounced as *estop* and *espell*. The problem here is entirely to do with the varying sound rules of the L1 and L2, and nothing to do with spelling. (For more details on such sound-driven problems caused by differences between the L1 and L2, see Appendix B.)

What can teachers do to minimise the influence of the spelling/pronunciation patterns and habits of L1 on their students' pronunciation of English? One approach is where teachers work on the pronunciation of a word or longer utterance orally, before showing students the written form. Giving students the written form before they have practised it orally can lead to incorrect pronunciation being carried over into subsequent oral practice.

Working on pronunciation before giving students a written record is fine within the controlled environment of the classroom, and in many instances both desirable and advantageous. However, giving students a written record in itself is not enough to help them remember the pronunciation unless the relatively complex links between English spelling and pronunciation have been made clear. Making these links will help students in their independent study away from the classroom. Teachers should therefore get into the regular habit of using phonemic symbols in combination with a written record of the language being practised, and make a point of drawing students' attention to the most important spelling/sound relationships.

Regular dictionary work is also to be encouraged, and students should be enabled to use a good dictionary which uses phonemic symbols. Teachers can do work in class to help students become more familiar with the dictionary, and to gain confidence in working out pronunciations from phonemic script.

In a multilingual class, there will be a variety of different types of mistakes, reflecting the pronunciation and spelling difficulties of the various L1s represented. In such classes, teachers need to develop an awareness of the difficulties specific to the individual L1s represented in the class, without making classroom activities too L1-specific. Activities can focus on spelling and pronunciation difficulties which arise from work on particular language structures, and which are relevant to the majority of students in that particular class. The aim should be to alert students to generalities that they can then apply in their own reading and writing. In monolingual classes, teachers can be more selective, choosing examples of mistakes which are typical for students for that particular L1, as well as addressing the more general challenges which the English spelling system presents.

Sample lessons The following sample lessons show some teaching ideas in action.

Lesson 1: Spelling of suffixes and the pronunciation of /ə/ (Intermediate to Advanced)

Lesson type: Integrated
Materials: List of words/list of suffixes

The class is working on vocabulary extension, through adding suffixes to words. The teacher starts by dividing the class into pairs or small groups. Then she writes the following lists (or similar) on the board, or gives them out on a handout to each group. (The best way to compile a list is to make the lesson a follow-on from previous work, like a reading comprehension text which has included some of the suffixes to be studied.)

List 1: wonder, suspect, manage, detect, write, interpret, home, success, instruct, protect, harm, pronounce, demonstrate, discuss, admire, survive, beauty, correct, communicate, politics, buy, thought, infect...

List 2: -er, -or, -ian, -ful, -ation, -tion, -icion, -ent, -less, -ion

Students work together in pairs or small groups to try to add suffixes from list 2 to the words on list 1 as appropriate. Some they may find relatively easy, and others will be more challenging; some involve a change in spelling (e.g. *pronounce–pronunciation*). The groups or pairs then compare answers, and the teacher checks the answers with the whole class, making sure that students have the opportunity to copy or note down the right answers. The teacher then asks the students to mark primary stresses on the words; she elicits a couple of examples from the class first, to make sure that everyone has the right idea, for example:

    ▢
wonderful   ▢
    detection

After the students have again had the time to discuss their answers, and after the teacher has checked these, she asks the students to mark all incidences of /ə/; it is useful to elicit a few examples, and perhaps drill the sound chorally a few times to make sure all the students understand the nature of the exercise. The teacher instructs the students to try saying the words to each other if they are not sure. Having compared their answers with other groups again, the teacher elicits the answers from the class, and marks (or invites the students to come to the board and mark) the incidences of /ə/. The teacher finally draws the students' attention to the fact that most (but not all) of the incidences of /ə/ fall on the suffixes, and that all of the suffixes contain one example of the sound. The lexical work in this type of activity can also be successfully tied in with work on word stress, as /ə/ will always be part of an unstressed syllable.

Lesson 2: Different spellings of vowel sounds (Pre-Intermediate)

Lesson type: Practice
Materials: Task sheet with two lists of words

The teacher can use activities like the one which follows to focus on particular sounds which have been causing students difficulties, either productively or receptively.

The activity itself is a simple matching exercise, where students match words which they think probably have the same vowel sound. The sounds given here in this example are /iː/, /e/, /ʊ/, /ɔː/, /ɑː/ and /ɜː/. Students are each given a task sheet with the following words on:

head	laugh
seize	girl
put	rent
sore	heat
heart	cook
heard	law

The teacher asks the students to work individually to match the words with the same sound; students then compare their answers, and the teacher conducts feedback. The words can, at any stage, be read out or played from a tape, depending on the approach the teacher feels is best suited to the class. The sounds can then be worked on in a variety of ways: the teacher can drill the words, drill the sounds, and take the opportunity, if students are not familiar with the relevant phonemic symbols, to introduce them at this stage. As a way of extending the activity, students can be asked to add more words with the same sounds, or to add more words with the same spellings. The activity could also be a dictionary-based one, with students finding the words in a good dictionary to help them match up the sounds.

Lesson 3: Wrong spelling test: Spelling/sound relationships (All levels)

Lesson type: Practice
Materials: List of words, some spelled correctly, others not. List is compiled from students' homework.

The teacher tells students that they are going to have a spelling test, based on words from their recent written work. She organises the students into pairs, and gives each pair a list of words. Some of the words are spelled correctly, and some are not. The students' task is to find the incorrect ones and to provide the correct version. The activity can be done competitively if you wish: pairs race to see who can finish first. When one pair has finished, the teacher checks to see if they have corrected appropriately. If they have not, then the race continues. An example list of words could be: *pichure, receipt, wonderfull, ensure, enoug, preferred, protecked, learnt, pronounciation, confuse.*

The words might also be included in a reading text, which students have to correct. It is important that the task is checked at class level, and tied in with pronunciation. Depending on the students' abilities, the teacher can also ask them to attempt an explanation for the wrong spellings, to say where the potential confusions are, and/or to use phonemic script to show how the word is pronounced.

Lesson 4: Dictionary work: Spelling/sound relationships (All levels)

Lesson type: Practice
Materials: Dictionaries. List of words, all including the sound being focused on

This example uses different possible pronunciations for the letter *o*, but the activity can, of course, be tailored to cover whatever practice the class needs.

The teacher gives the students a selection of words which include the letter *o*. For example: *song, donkey, love, comfortable, nothing, done, hot, monkey, Monday, gone, son, across, annoy, brother, won.*

Students are asked to work in pairs, and with the help of a dictionary to categorise the words according to how the letter *o* is pronounced in each one. The pairs try to see how many different pronunciations they can find. The activity can be made competitive, with pairs racing to complete the categorisation. To make the task easier for students who are not so confident with pronunciation work, phonemic symbols showing the different possible pronunciations of *o* can be given to them. Activities like this will increase students' confidence in their predictions of the relationships between spelling and sounds, and also help them to increase their understanding and knowledge of the spelling and pronunciation systems. Guided work in using dictionaries to find pronunciations will also help students take a more independent role in their awareness of pronunciation in private study away from the classroom.

Dictionary work can also be done with reading texts as a way of extending a comprehension task. Students can be asked, for example, to find all the words containing /iː/ in the text, or any other sound which needs attention. Students will often be able to predict many of these, but can use the dictionaries to look up the ones they are not sure about.

Lesson 5: 'Trevor's day': Present simple tense, final *s* as /s/ or /z/ (Elementary)

Lesson type: Integrated
Materials: A set of drawings or photos of the events in Trevor's day (optional)

The primary aim of the lesson is to introduce the 3rd person verb forms for a set of verbs, but the pronunciation of the verb endings is also relevant. The teacher uses drawings or photos to elicit and drill facts about the daily habits of a real or imaginary person. For example:

Trevor lives in Burnley.	He eats his breakfast.
He gets up at 6 o'clock each morning.	He reads his newspaper.
He has a shower.	He cycles to work.

Having drilled the sentences chorally and individually, the teacher gives students an activity to practise recognising and using them. For example, students can be given a series of pictures representing Trevor's typical day, which they have to put in the correct order. Or, to make the exercise more communicative, they can be given information (or visual prompts) about the daily habits of another person; students work in pairs to exchange information, building up a picture of the subject's typical day.

The teacher then writes on the board two or three of the verbs which have appeared in each sentence, says them out loud, and asks the students if they notice any pronunciation difference at the end. He elicits the fact that some have an /s/ sound, while some have /z/. (The rule is that /s/ will be said after an unvoiced consonant sound, and /z/ after a voiced consonant or vowel/diphthong.) Once the point has been made, the teacher asks students to categorise the other verbs on the list; students can be given a task sheet with the verb forms and a column each for /s/ and /z/, or the columns can be put on the board, and students can be invited to the board to do the categorisation.

The level of detail used in the explanation depends on previous work done with the class. It is perfectly possible at elementary level to introduce and use terms like 'voiced' and 'voiceless', to help students discover more about the pronunciation of English. If the students are comfortable with these terms (or alternative descriptions, like 'use your voice', and 'don't use your voice'), then the rule can be explained. Teachers might simply want to use the opportunity to bring up the idea that some 3rd person singular present simple verb forms are pronounced with /s/ and some with /z/. Whatever the level of detail used, the lesson helps students to practise the pronunciation of the endings, as well as helping them to remember to add a final letter s when writing.

The teacher can follow up the pronunciation focus by asking students to work in pairs in order to tell each other about their own typical day. Students can then form new pairs, using the 3rd person forms to tell their new partner about the student they have just been working with. The speaking exercises can then be followed up with a written exercise, where students write about a person they know, a famous person or celebrity, or an imaginary person, again with the idea of practising the 3rd person forms.

Conclusions In this chapter we have noted that English is not a 'phonetic' language but, despite the seeming complexity of the English spelling system, there is still a high degree of regularity. We have seen that the patterns of spelling can provide a useful opportunity for helping students to improve their pronunciation and spelling at the same time.

We have seen that:
• pronunciation and spelling are very much interconnected, and that habits and generalisations from L1 may be brought over into L2.

And we have concluded that:
• working on spelling and pronunciation together helps students' independent study outside the classroom.

Task File

Introduction

- The exercises in this section all relate to topics discussed in the chapter to which the exercises refer. Some expect definite answers while others ask only for the reader's ideas and opinions.

- Tutors can decide when it is appropriate to use the tasks in this section. Readers on their own can work on the tasks at any stage in their reading of the book.

- An answer key (pages 141–142) is provided after the Task File for those tasks where it is possible to provide specific or suggested answers. The symbol [☞] beside an exercise indicates that answers are given for that exercise in the answer key.

- The material in the Task File can be photocopied for use in limited circumstances. Please see the notice on the back of the title page for the restrictions on photocopying.

The description of speech

A Phonemes   Page 1

Write the phonemic symbols for the underlined parts of the words, marking unvoiced consonants with (U). Two examples have been done. (Check your answers against the table on page 2.)

Vowels		Diphthongs		Consonants		
i:	b<u>ea</u>d		c<u>a</u>ke	p (U)	<u>p</u>in	<u>s</u>ue
	h<u>i</u>t		t<u>oy</u>		<u>b</u>in	<u>z</u>oo
	b<u>oo</u>k		h<u>igh</u>		<u>t</u>o	<u>sh</u>e
	f<u>oo</u>d		b<u>ee</u>r		<u>d</u>o	mea<u>s</u>ure
	l<u>e</u>ft		f<u>ewe</u>r		<u>c</u>ot	<u>h</u>ello
	<u>a</u>bout		wh<u>ere</u>		<u>g</u>ot	<u>m</u>ore
	sh<u>ir</u>t		g<u>o</u>		<u>ch</u>urch	<u>n</u>o
	c<u>a</u>ll		h<u>ouse</u>		<u>j</u>udge	si<u>ng</u>
	h<u>a</u>t				<u>f</u>an	<u>l</u>ive
	r<u>u</u>n				<u>v</u>an	<u>r</u>ed
	f<u>ar</u>				<u>th</u>ink	<u>y</u>es
	d<u>o</u>g				<u>th</u>e	<u>w</u>ood

B The articulation of consonants   Page 6

Put **a, b** etc. in each box to match the consonant sound classifications (**a–d**) to the sound characteristics (**1–4**).

a plosives   **b** fricatives   **c** approximants   **d** lateral

1 The articulators come close together, but do not cause audible friction.	
2 A closure is made in the vocal tract and air flows around the sides of the tongue.	
3 A complete closure is made in the vocal tract and the air is then released explosively.	
4 Air is heard passing between two vocal organs.	

C Phonemic transcription   Page 7

Bad elephant jokes. Match the punchlines (**a–e**) to the relevant questions.

1 /wɒt taɪm ɪz ɪt wen ən elɪfənt sɪts ɒn jə fens/	**a** /ðeərə fʊtprɪnts ɪn ðe bʌtə/
2 /haʊ də jə get daʊn frəm ən elɪfənt/	**b** /ɪt sɪts ɒn ə liːf ən weɪts tɪl ɔːtəm/
3 /haʊ də jə nəʊ ɪf ən elɪfənt əz bɪn ɪn jə frɪdʒ/	**c** /jə hæf tə get daʊn frəm ə dʌk/
4 /haʊ duː elɪfənts meɪk ɔːl ðeə fəʊn kɔːlz/	**d** /taɪm tə get ə njuː wʌn/
5 /haʊ dəz ən elɪfənt get daʊn frəm ə triː/	**e** /trʌŋk əv kɔːs/

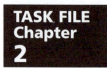

TASK FILE Chapter 2

Teaching pronunciation

☞ **A Including pronunciation in lesson planning** Pages 12 and 23

Consider the following structures. Analyse them in terms of pronunciation features. The first is done as an example. One example sentence is also given for the other structures; you will need to add some more. In the final row, analyse the pronunciation of a structure for a lesson you will be teaching soon.

Structure	Pronunciation features
1 Comparative and superlative adjectives: *Chris is taller than Tim.* *Tim is not as tall as Mike.* *Mike is the tallest.*	/ə/ appears in 'than' and 'as'. '-er' is pronounced as /ə/. '-est' is pronounced as /ɪst/. Contraction of 'Tim is...' to 'Tim's' /tɪmz/. Also 'Mike's' /maɪks/.
2 *Going to* futures: *They're going to emigrate.*	
3 Invitations using *Would you like to* + verb: *Would you like to come to my party?*	
4	

☞ **B Minimal pairs** Page 18

1 Which of the following pairs are minimal pairs? Which are not? Put a tick or a cross as relevant.

a	ship	sheep	✓	**f**	kite	coat	☐
b	cat	car	✗	**g**	bought	boat	☐
c	cheap	chip	☐	**h**	hit	heat	☐
d	heart	hear	☐	**i**	trick	treat	☐
e	cat	cut	☐	**j**	bins	beans	☐

2 Provide minimal pairs for the following phoneme difficulties.

Phonemes	Word pair		Phonemes	Word pair
/p/ and /b/	pin bin		/ɒ/ and /ɔː/	
/b/ and /v/			/e/ and /eɪ/	
/l/ and /r/			/ɪ/ and /iː/	
/θ/ and /s/			/ʊ/ and /uː/	
/dʒ/ and /j/			/æ/ and /ʌ/	

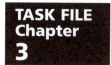

Vowels

A The characteristics of the 'pure' vowel sounds Page 29

Supply an example word for each sound. Mark the diagram
to show the tongue position. One has been done for you.
(Check your answers against the tables in Chapter 3.)

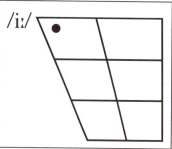

/iː/	bead	/ɜː/	
/ɪ/		·/ɔː/	
/ʊ/		/æ/	
/uː/		/ʌ/	
/e/		/ɑː/	
/ə/		/ɒ/	

B Raising awareness of vowel sounds Page 37

Start compiling a list of the vowel sounds your students have difficulty with, and list
ways in which you might explain how to create the sounds (see the table of suggestions
on page 38). Use the following headings:

Sound	Example words	Possible simple explanations
/ʌ/	cut, hut	Make the sound and throw your head back slightly.

C Planning a Practice lesson Page 40

Work alone or with a colleague to plan a two-part Practice lesson which includes work
on /æ/ and /ʌ/ (or any other pair of sounds which causes difficulties for your students).
Here is a table of options you might consider using.

Sounds	First part	Second part
/æ/ and /ʌ/ /ɪ/ and /iː/ etc.	Drilling Minimal pairs Listening Activity etc.	Phonemic bingo Phonemic 'Snap' Collaborative writing Reading aloud etc.

Consonants

A **Consonant sounds**   Page 48

Provide three words for each consonant phoneme, with the sound at the beginning, middle and end of the word. The 'impossible' one has been blocked out.

	Beginning	Middle	End			Beginning	Middle	End
p	/pen/				z			
	pen		wasp					
k					3			

B **Raising awareness of consonant sounds**   Page 54

1 Insert the appropriate consonant sound for each 'learner-friendly' description. Bear in mind that for voiced and unvoiced 'pairs', one description will do. The first one is done for you.

Sound(s)	'Learner-friendly' descriptions
a /θ/ & /ð/	Put the front of your tongue against the back of your top teeth. Let the air pass through as you breathe out. Don't use your voice. Hold the sound, and add your voice.
b	Put your lips together. Use your voice, and let the air escape through your nose.
c	Put your lips together. Try to breathe out, but don't let the air escape. Release the air suddenly. Don't use your voice. Try again, and add your voice.
d	Open your mouth and breathe out. Don't use your voice, but try to make a noise.

2 Make a list of consonant difficulties your students seem to have. Think of ways of helping your students overcome the difficulties. Here is an example:

Problem	Solution
Jutta uses /v/ instead of /w/.	I could ask her to purse her lips as though about to whistle. I could then ask her to add her voice, and move on to a vowel sound (e.g. /ə/).

C **Lesson planning**   Page 58

Plan a two-part Practice lesson which includes work on consonant sounds which cause difficulties for your students. Try to incorporate a game or fun activity in the second part, as in this example:

Sounds/L1	First part	Second part
/p/ Arabic	Minimal pairs (e.g. *pat* and *bat*) activity	Creating advertising slogans that include /p/ as much as possible.

**TASK FILE
Chapter
5**

Word and sentence stress

A What is word stress? What is unstress? Page 66

1 Number the words with the appropriate stress pattern (1–5). Two examples are done for you.

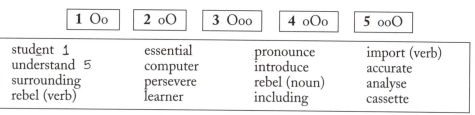

| 1 Oo | 2 oO | 3 Ooo | 4 oOo | 5 ooO |

stud<u>e</u>nt 1	essential	pronounce	import (verb)
understand 5	computer	introduce	accurate
surrounding	persevere	rebel (noun)	analyse
rebel (verb)	learner	including	cassette

2 Using the words above, underline all the incidences of /ə/. (See the word *student* above.) What vowel sounds other than /ə/ also appear in the unstressed syllables?

B Sentence stress and tonic syllables Page 71

Listen to the utterances (1–5) below on the CD. Match them to the possible meanings (**a–e**). Tonic syllables are shown in capitals and underlined.

94

Utterances	Possible meanings
1 <u>I'LL</u> walk with you to the station.	**a** I don't want to bring my car.
2 I'll <u>WALK</u> with you to the station.	**b** But not back again.
3 I'll walk with <u>YOU</u> to the station.	**c** But not as far as the park.
4 I'll walk with you <u>TO</u> the station.	**d** But I'm not going with him.
5 I'll walk with you to the <u>STA</u>tion.	**e** Nobody else has offered.

C Weak forms Page 73

Listen to the following sentences on the CD. Write the phonemic transcription of the underlined words as they are pronounced.

95

1 What <u>am</u> I doing? _____   5 I'll see you <u>at</u> the party. _____
2 Yes, I <u>am</u>. _____   6 What are you looking <u>at</u>? _____
3 Those shoes <u>are</u> lovely! _____   7 I <u>can</u> swim faster than you! _____
4 Yes, they <u>are</u>. _____   8 Oh yes I <u>can</u>! _____

D Raising awareness of word and sentence stress Page 75

Plan an Integrated lesson for Pre-Intermediate students on a language issue (e.g. future forms, or comparatives) which can include work on sentence stress. Work out examples of the language, and plan how you will deal with grammar (and lexis) and stress. Here is an example:

Language	Activity	Examples with stresses in capitals
Past simple	Role-play where students have different information about the same event.	JOHN WENT to the CINema. He WENT to the THEatre, NOT the CINema.

TASK FILE Chapter 6

Intonation

A Tones, tonic syllables and tone units Page 88

Listen to these five sentences on the CD. Tone groups are already marked. Rewrite them indicating the onset syllable (if appropriate) and the tonic syllable, and indicating if the tone movement is a fall, or a fall-rise.

(96)

1 //im sorry//but i really dont know// _____

2 //is this going to go here//or there// _____

3 //thats another big bill weve got to pay// _____

4 //that letters for you//and this ones for me// _____

5 //id like to offer you the job// _____

B Teaching the intonation of question tags Page 89

Plan an Integrated lesson which includes intonation work on question tags with Intermediate students. Work out examples of the language, and plan how you will deal with intonation, grammar and lexis.

C Discourse and intonation Page 101

Tick the sentence if you think it indicates common ground (i.e. previously shared knowledge) between the speakers, and a cross if not. Try saying the sentences, or listen to them on the CD.

(97)

1 // ↘WHATS your <u>NAME</u>//

2 // ↗WHATS your <u>NAME</u>//

3 // ↗WHAT colour is your <u>CAR</u>//

4 // ↘WHAT colour is your <u>CAR</u>//

5 // ↘youre <u>FRENCH</u>// ↘<u>ARENT</u> you

6 // ↘youre <u>FRENCH</u>// ↗<u>ARENT</u> you

D Analysing intonation Page 105

If resources are available, tape yourself and a student talking for a short time about the same topics. Don't script your speech, but agree on basic content, and the order of that content. Suggested content is as follows:

- Your name.
- How old you are.
- Where you come from.
- Where you live.
- What you do.
- How long you have been teaching/learning English.
- How many people there are in your family, and what their names are.

Have a couple of trial runs before you record yourselves. Try to speak as naturally as possible. Then analyse (either for your own study, or with your student) your parallel talks for intonation use, and consider the intonation issues you should work on with your students.

TASK FILE
Chapter
7

Other aspects of connected speech

☞ **A Assimilation**   Page 109

Decide what the assimilations are in the following sentences.

(98) 1 It's in that box. _The /t/ at the end of 'that' assimilates to_ _____

2 There are eleven players in a soccer team._____

3 Can you see that kid over there? _____

4 There are ten cups on the table. _____

5 I'm going to give up smoking this year._____

☞ **B Elision**   Page 110

Decide what the elisions are in the following sentences.

(99) 1 We finally arrived the next day.   _/nekst/ becomes_ _____

2 This is Everton's last chance to win the league. _____

3 We had a cold lunch in a small bar. _____

4 If you visit Britain, you must try some fish and chips. _____

5 Her mum always served sherry on Christmas morning._____

☞ **C Linking and intrusion**   Page 111

Decide which sound intrudes or links sounds in the following sentences.

1 It was an important media event.   _/r/ intrudes between_ _____

2 You can park the car over there. _____

3 Trevor's weird. He eats raw onion for breakfast._____

4 He was way over the speed limit. _____

5 Did you go out on New Year's Eve? _____

D Awareness of aspects of connected speech   Pages 109–113

Make a list of ten different sentences you have practised with your classes recently.
Analyse these sentences for examples of:

• Assimilation	• Elision
• Linking sounds	• Intrusive /r/
• Weak forms	• Contractions

E Teaching aspects of connected speech   Page 116

Plan an Integrated lesson for Elementary students which includes work on aspects of
connected speech. Choose a language point from an elementary coursebook, and plan
how you will deal with examples of elision, assimilation etc, as well as grammar and
lexis.

Pronunciation and spelling

☞ A Regular features of pronunciation   Page 123

1 Look at the following lists of words. Each list includes a particular combination of letters. How many different sounds can you find represented in each list?

ea	ch	ou	ei
beach	microchip	flout	height
break	machine	trouble	perceive
weather	mechanic	cough	reign
learn		boulder	heir
bear		soup	heifer
near		thought	heist
hearth		tour	

2 Letters in environments (page 124 and Table 8 on page 152)
Comment on the role played by the letters (*e*, *y* etc.) in the following words.

    a *e*: hat/hate   <u>The addition of the 'e' makes the vowel letter 'say its name'.</u>

    b *y*: tin/tiny   _____

    c *r*: ham/harm   _____

    d *w*: not/now   _____

3 Root and derived words (page 125)
Transcribe the root and derived word. Notice the sound changes.

    a sign   ____/saɪn/____   signal   ____/'sɪgnəl/____

    b invite   _____   invitation   _____

    c courage   _____   courageous   _____

    d photograph   _____   photographer   _____

B Teaching pronunciation and spelling

1 Analyse some samples of your students' recent written work for spelling mistakes. Categorise the mistakes according to the following criteria:

    a The student doesn't know how to spell the word.
    b This is a slip; the student would normally spell the word correctly.
    c There is a link with pronunciation. The student isn't aware which letters to use to represent the sounds.

2 Make a list of recent pronunciation mistakes your students have made in class. Categorise the mistakes according to the following criteria:

    a This was a new word. The student wasn't aware how to pronounce it.
    b This was a slip. The student normally pronounces this correctly.
    c There is a link with spelling. The student tried to pronounce this word as it is written.

3 Plan a Practice lesson (P) to deal with some of the mistakes you have noted. See if you can devise a game which will help clarify any areas of difficulty.

Task File Key

Chapter 1

B 1 c
  2 d
  3 a
  4 b

C 1 d
  2 c
  3 a
  4 e
  5 b

Chapter 2

A2 *Going to* futures: *to* is pronounced /tə/ (weak form) when followed by a consonant sound. When followed by a vowel sound, it is pronounced as /tuː/ (full form). Students may also come across *going to* pronounced as *gonna* /gɒnə/ or /gʌnə/.

A3 Invitations using *Would you like to* + verb: *Would you* is often pronounced as /ˈwʊdʒə/. *To* is pronounced with the weak form /tə/ before a consonant sound, and with the full form /tuː/ before a vowel sound.

B1 c ✓   d ✗   e ✓   f ✓
   g ✓   h ✓   i ✗   j ✓

B2 /b/ and /v/   ban van   /e/ and /eɪ/   get gate
   /l/ and /r/   late rate   /ɪ/ and /iː/   lick leak
   /θ/ and /s/   think sink   /ʊ/ and /uː/   look Luke
   /dʒ/ and /j/ jaw your   /æ/ and /ʌ/   cat cut
   /ɒ/ and /ɔː/ cot caught

Chapter 4

A   /p/ pen happen wasp   /z/ zoo houses goes
    /k/ cart flicker talk   /ʒ/ pleasure beige

B1 **b** /m/   **c** /p/ and /b/   **d** /h/

Chapter 5

A1/2 (Incidences of /ə/ are underlined.)
        stud<u>e</u>nt 1   pr<u>o</u>nounce 2
        und<u>e</u>rstand 5   intr<u>o</u>duce 5
        s<u>u</u>rrounding 4   reb<u>e</u>l (noun) 1
        rebel (verb) 2   including 4
        essenti<u>a</u>l 4   import (verb) 2
        comput<u>e</u>r 4   acc<u>u</u>rate 3
        pers<u>e</u>vere 5   an<u>a</u>lyse 3
        learn<u>e</u>r 1   c<u>a</u>ssette 2

B 1 e   2 a   3 d   4 b   5 c

C 1 /əm/   2 /æm/   3 /ə/   4 /ɑː/
   5 /ət/   6 /æt/   7 /kən/   8 /kæn/

Chapter 6

A 1 // ⌄ im SORry// ↘ but i REALly dont KNOW//
   2 // ⌄ is THIS going to go HERE// ↘ or THERE//
   3 // ↘ THATS aNOther big bill weve got to pay//
   4 // ⌄ THAT letters for YOU// ↘ and THIS ones for ME//
   5 // ↘ id LIKE to offer you the JOB//

C 1 ✗ 2 ✓ 3 ✓ 4 ✗ 5 ✓ 6 ✗

Chapter 7

A 1 /t/ assimilates to /p/
   2 /n/ assimilates to /m/
   3 /t/ assimilates to /k/
   4 /n/ assimilates to /ŋ/
   5 /s/ assimilates to /ʃ/

B 1 /nekst/ becomes /neks/; the /t/ is lost
   2 /t/ is lost
   3 /d/ is lost
   4 /t/ is lost and /d/ is lost
   5 /d/ is lost

C 1 /r/ intrudes between *media* and *event*
   2 /r/ links *car* and *over*.
   3 /r/ intrudes between *raw* and *onion*
   4 /j/ links *way* and *over*
   5 /w/ links *go* and *out*

Chapter 8

A1 *ea*: /iː/ /eɪ/ /e/ /ɜː/ /eə/ /ɪə/ /ɑː/
    ch: /tʃ/ /ʃ/ /k/
    ou: /aʊ/ /ʌ/ /ɒ/ /əʊ/ /uː/ /ɔː/ /ʊə/
    ei: /aɪ/ /iː/ /eɪ/ /eə/ /e/ /aɪ/

A2 **b** The addition of *y* makes the vowel *i* 'say its name'.
    c The addition of *r* turns the short sound /æ/ into the long sound /ɑː/.
    d Changing *t* to *w* turns /ɒ/ into /aʊ/.

A3 **b** /ɪnˈvaɪt/   /ɪnvɪˈteɪʃən/
    c /ˈkʌrɪdʒ/   /kəˈreɪdʒəs/
    d /ˈfəʊtəgrɑːf/   /fəˈtɒgrəfə/

Appendix A

Learners' reference chart of English sounds

Consonants

Front ← → Back

How to make the sound: Don't use your voice (shaded) / Use your voice

What happens?	Put both lips together	Use top teeth and bottom lip	Use tongue behind top teeth	Touch bump behind teeth with tongue	Between ←→	Hard bit of the roof of mouth	Touch roof of mouth (the soft bit) with your tongue	Use your throat
Stop air. Let it go suddenly	p b			t d			k g	
Stop air. Let it go gradually					tʃ dʒ			
Let air pass through		f v	θ ð	s z	ʃ ʒ			h
Let air out of your nose	m			n			ŋ	
Air goes round tongue				l				
Nearly touching	(w)				r	j	w	

Vowels

Tongue: Low ↔ High

Front ← → Back

iː	ɪ	ʊ	uː
e	ə	ɜː	ɔː
æ	ʌ	ɑː	ɒ

Lips can be:

Spread	Neutral	Rounded

Diphthongs

End at front → End at back

Closing	Centring	Closing
eɪ	ɪə	əʊ
ɔɪ	ʊə	aʊ
aɪ	eə	

Intonation & Stress

Fall	↘
Fall/Rise	↘↗
Rise	↗
Rise/Fall	↗↘
Level	→

Primary stress ˈ

Secondary stress ˌ

Appendix B

Common pronunciation difficulties

This appendix outlines the main phoneme difficulties which speakers of particular languages can have when speaking English.

Key to languages: A=Arabic; C=Chinese; F=French; G=German; Gk=Greek; Ind=Indian languages; It=Italian; J=Japanese; P=Portuguese; R=Russian; Sc=Scandinavian languages; Sp=Spanish; Tu=Turkish

Consonants

Sound	Potential Difficulty — Can be pronounced		A	C	F	G	Gk	Ind	It	J	P	R	Sc	Sp	Tu
p	/b/	/ben/ for *pen*	•					•			•	•		•	
b	/p/	/pɪn/ for *bin*	•												
	/p/	at end of words		•		•						•	•	•	
t	/d/	/dɪn/ for *tin*						•				•			
	/tʃ/	/tʃiːm/ for *team*								•	•				
	/ts/	/tsuː/ for *too*								•					
d	/t/	/tɪn/ for *din*						•			•				
	/dʒ/	/dʒiːp/ for *deep*								•	•				
	/t/	at end of words		•		•						•	•	•	
		like /ð/												•	
k	/g/	/gɒt/ for *cot*	•					•			•	•		•	
		can be omitted at end of words												•	
g	/k/	/kɒt/ for *got*	•												
	/k/	at end of words		•		•						•	•	•	
	/ʒ/	/ˈʒetɪŋ/ for *getting*									•				
		gutturally												•	
tʃ	/ʃ/	/kæʃ/ for *catch*	•	•	•		•				•			•	
dʒ	/ʒ/	/ˈmeɪʒə/ for *major*	•		•		•				•			•	
	/tʃ/	/tʃuːn/ for *June*		•		•									•
f		a bit like /h/								•					
v	/f/	/fæn/ for *van*	•	•		•									
	/w/	/wæn/ for *van*		•		•			•						•
	/b/	/bæn/ for *van*								•				•	
θ	/s/	/sɪŋ/ for *thing*	•	•	•	•				•	•	•	•		•
	/t/	/tɪn/ for *thin*		•	•			•	•		•		•		•
	/f/	/fɪn/ for′ *thin*		•	•										

Potential Difficulty		For speakers of:												
Sound	**Can be pronounced**	**A**	**C**	**F**	**G**	**Gk**	**Ind**	**It**	**J**	**P**	**R**	**Sc**	**Sp**	**Tu**
ð	/z/ /zɪs/ for *this*	•	•	•	•				•	•	•			•
	/d/ /deə/ for *there*		•	•			•	•		•		•		•
	/v/ /væt/ for *that*		•	•										
s	/ʃ/ /ʃiː/ for *see*								•					
z	/s/ /gəʊs/ for *goes*	•	•	•	•	•	•	•	•	•	•	•	•	•
	/dʒ/ /dʒɪp/ for *zip*								•					
ʃ	/s/ /sɒp/ for *shop*		•			•								
	/tʃ/ /tʃɒp/ for *shop*												•	
ʒ	/ʃ/ /ˈpleʃə/ for *pleasure*	•	•		•	•		•		•			•	
h	gutturally	•	•			•				•	•		•	
	sound dropped/put in inappropriately			•				•		•			•	
	a bit like /f/								•					
m	like /ŋ/ at end of words												•	
n	not a phoneme (some dialects)		•											
ŋ	followed by /g/ or /k/ /sɪŋk/ for *sing*	•		•	•	•		•		•				•
l	/r/ /rent/ for *lent*		•						•					
	like /ʊ/ at end of word		•						•	•				
r	articulated differently	•	•	•	•		•		•	•		•	•	
	/l/ /lent/ for *rent*		•						•					
j	/dʒ/ /dʒes/ for *yes*												•	
w	/v/ /vaɪn/ for *wine*			•		•				•	•			•
	either as /b/ or /gw/												•	
	Vowel insertion in consonant clusters e.g. /seterˈɒŋ/ for *strong*	•	•				•		•	•			•	•

Vowels and diphthongs

Potential Difficulty		For speakers of:												
Sound	**Can be pronounced**	**A**	**C**	**F**	**G**	**Gk**	**Ind**	**It**	**J**	**P**	**R**	**Sc**	**Sp**	**Tu**
iː	/ɪ/ /hɪt/ for *heat*		•			•				•	•			•
ɪ	/e/ /bed/ for *bid*	•												
	/iː/ /hiːt/ for *hit*		•	•		•		•	•	•		•	•	•
ʊ	/uː/ /puːl/ for *pull*		•			•		•		•			•	•
uː	/ʊ/ /sʊt/ for *suit*		•							•				
e	/ɪ/ /bɪd/ for *bed*	•					•							•
ə	in various ways	•	•	•	•	•	•	•	•	•	•	•	•	•
ɜː	/ɑː/ /bɑːd/ for *bird*								•					

Potential Difficulty		For speakers of:												
Sound	Can be pronounced	A	C	F	G	Gk	Ind	It	J	P	R	Sc	Sp	Tu
ɔː	/ɒ/ /tɒt/ for *taught*	•	•	•	•	•			•	•	•		•	•
	/əʊ/ /kəʊt/ for *caught*		•	•	•			•			•			•
	/ɑː/ /kɑːt/ for *caught*						•							
æ	/ɑː/ /hɑːt/ for *hat*		•			•		•	•	•	•		•	•
	/e/ /set/ for *sat*	•		•	•		•	•		•	•	•		
	/ʌ/ /kʌt/ for *cat*	•				•							•	
ʌ	/æ/ /fæn/ for *fun*	•	•			•			•	•	•		•	•
	/ɜː/ /lɜːv/ for *love*			•										
	/ʊ/ /lʊk/ for *luck*			•		•			•		•		•	
ɑː	/æ/ /kænt/ for *can't*	•	•	•	•	•	•	•	•	•	•		•	•
ɒ	/ɑː/ /pɑːt/ for *pot*						•							
eɪ	/e/ /pled/ for *played*			•	•		•	•				•		
ɔɪ	/aɪ/ /baɪ/ for *boy*						•							
aɪ														
ɪə	Final ə may present problems for many	*Many diphthongs simplified*	*Many diphthongs simplified*	•	•	•	•	•	•	•	•	•	*Second part of diphthong emphasised*	*Many diphthongs simplified*
ʊə				•	•	•	•	•	•	•	•	•		
eə	/ɪə/ /tʃɪə/ for *chair*									•				
əʊ	/ɒ/ /kɒp/ for *cope*			•		•		•	•	•				
	/ɔː/ /kɔːt/ for *coat*			•		•		•	•	•				
aʊ														

Appendix C

Spelling and pronunciation tables

Tables 1 to 5 analyse the links between the spelling and the pronunciation of consonants. Tables 6 to 7 analyse vowel letters and sounds, and Table 8 looks at the interplay of vowels and consonants. Where there is significant variation in 'General American' English (the standard form in the USA), this is noted in the tables. 'G.A.' is used here as an abbreviation.

Table 1: 'Simple' consonants

The following consonants have one main sound association.

Letter	Sound	Examples
b	/b/	*beach, cabbage, cab*
d	/d/	*do, oddity, cod*
f	/f/	*for, coffee, off*
h	/h/	*hello, behind*
j	/dʒ/	*judge, major*
k	/k/	*kick, making, take*
l	/l/	*leg, hello, poll*
m	/m/	*me, coming, plum*
n	/n/	*no, any, plain*
r	/r/	*run, carrot*
s	/s/	*sit, missing, kiss*
t	/t/	*tub, butter, but* (Letter *t* between vowel sounds is often voiced in G.A.)
v	/v/	*very, having, brave*
w	/w/	*we, towards*
z	/z/	*zebra, lizard, maze*

Some of the above letters do have alternative sounds, but they tend to be restricted to one or two words, like the /v/ sound of *f* in *of*. Notice also that when the above letters are doubled (as in *letter, cabbage, coffee* etc.) the sound does not change.

Table 2: 'Silent' consonants

The following letters appear in spellings where they are not actually pronounced.

Letter	Silent in
b	*su**b**tle, dou**b**t, clim**b***
c	*s**c**issors, s**c**ene, mus**c**le*
d	*We**d**nesday, san**d**wich, han**d**kerchief*
g	*__g__naw, ou__g__ht, lon__g__*
h	*__h__our, w__h__at, oug__h__t*
k	*__k__now, __k__nee*
l	*ta__l__k, ha__l__f, cou__l__d*
n	*autum__n__, colum__n__*
p	*__p__sychology, __p__neumonia, cu__p__board, recei__p__t*
r	*ca__r__, mo__r__e, co__r__e, bothe__r__* (in non-rhotic accents)
s	*i__s__land, ai__s__le*
t	*lis__t__en, whis__t__le, of__t__en* (though some speakers pronounce it in *often*)
w	*__w__rite, __w__rong, t__w__o, ans__w__er, yello__w__*

Table 3: Consonants with different 'flavours'

Some consonants can be pronounced in different ways. (There are exceptions to the rules here, but the following examples illustrate the most common alternative pronunciations.)

Letter	Alternative pronunciations	
c	/k/	*cat*
	/s/	when followed by *e, i* or *y*: *cent, cinema, cycle*
	/ʃ/	before certain suffixes: *delicious, prejudicial*
g	/g/	*go*
	/dʒ/	when followed by *e, i,* or *y*: *gentle, gin, gym, refrigerate* (Some exceptions are very common words: *get, give* and *girl*.)
	/dʒ/	before a suffix: *contagious, prestigious*
	/ʒ/	in certain originally borrowed words: *prestige, mirage*
s	/s/	*sun, sleep, loss, eats, sleeps*
	/z/	when between two vowels: *present, losing*
	/z/	at the end of a word, after a voiced consonant (*hands, minds*), or after a vowel (*loses, houses*)
	/ʃ/	between a consonant and a following *i*: *mansion, pension*
	/ʒ/	between two vowels: *vision, measure, lesion*
t	/t/	*cat, too*
	/ʃ/	when followed by a letter *i* in many suffixed words: *information, substantial, ambitious*
	/tʃ/	in words ending in *-ure* (*picture, furniture, denture*) and when followed by the sound /uː/ (*Tuesday, tumour, tumultuous*)

x	/ks/	*fix, mix, fixture, mixture*
	/gz/	between vowels: *exam, exact*
	/z/	at the beginning of words like *xylophone* and *xenophobe*
y	/j/	at the beginning of words: *yes, yellow*
	/ɪ/	between consonants: *gym, bicycle*
	/iː/	at end of words: *city, busy* (In connected speech this can be pronounced as /ɪ/.)
	/aɪ/	in short words (*why, my, by*) and in stressed final syllables (*apply, deny*)
	/aɪ/	in words ending in *-fy* (*satisfy, beautify*) and in *gynaecology, psychology* and related words.
		Helps form diphthongs in *boy, gay, buy, obey* etc.

Table 4: Double consonants

Most doubled consonants do not change from their single sound value (e.g. *rub, rubber, fat, fatter, thin, thinner*). The following doubles, however, can undergo the changes described below:

cc	/ks/	when followed by *e* or *i*: *success, accident, succinct*
	/tʃ/	in borrowed Italian words: *cappuccino*
gg	/dʒ/	when followed by *e* or *i*: *suggest, exaggerate*
ss	/ʃ/	when followed by *-ion* (*passion, permission*) and *-ure* (*pressure*)
zz	/ts/	in some borrowed Italian words: *pizza, mozzarella*

Table 5: Consonant digraphs/other combinations

Digraphs are two letters which represent one sound in a word. Some digraphs have more than one sound value.

ck	/k/	*pick, kick, pickle*
ch	/tʃ/	*chip, change*
	/k/	*character, technique*
	/ʃ/	*machine*
gh	/g/	*ghost, ghastly*
	/f/	*tough, cough*
	silent	*ought, though*
ng	/ŋ/	*sing, thing, singing*
ph	/f/	*phone, photograph, graphology*
qu	/kw/	*queen, quiz, antiquated*
	/k/	in a word ending in *-que* (*antique, oblique*) or at the beginning of some borrowed words (*quiche*)
sh	/ʃ/	*ship, sheep, cash, fashion*
tch	/tʃ/	*watch, catch, matching* (This is a trigraph.)
th	/θ/	*theatre, bath*
	/ð/	*this, brother, bathe*
wh	/w/	*what, where, nowhere*
	/h/	*who, whole*

Table 6: The 'basic menu' of vowel letters

The five vowel letters may be seen to have their most basic sounds when they occur in very short words, between two single consonant letters. Some dialects of English may have other variations to the ones listed here.

Letter	Pronounced as	
a	/æ/	*cat, hat, fat*
	/ɑː/	in RP and Southern British English before some two-consonant letter combinations: *bath, grass* but not before others: *bank, mass*
e	/e/	*let, met, set*
i	/ɪ/	*sit, lit, kit*
o	/ɒ/	*hot, got, lot* (*o* is pronounced as /ɑː/ in G.A.)
u	/ʌ/	*cup, bus, hut*

Table 7: Vowel digraphs/other combinations

English has a number of vowel digraphs where two vowel letters 'take the name' of the first letter, e.g. *ai* is pronounced /eɪ/ like the letter *A* . Most vowel digraphs have more than one sound associated with them – some have many more than one.

Letter	Pronounced as			
ai	/eɪ/	*raid, train*		
ea	/iː/	*dream, neat*	/eə/	*bear, tear* (verb)
	/eɪ/	*break, great*	/ɪə/	*near, tear* (noun)
	/e/	*dead, ready*	/ɑː/	*heart, hearth*
	/ɜː/	*learn, heard*		
ee	/iː/	*tree, need*	/ɪ/	weak form as in *been* /bɪn/
ei	/iː/	*seize, either, receive*	/eɪ/	*eight, reign*
	/aɪ/	*height, either*		
ie	/aɪ/	*die, pie, cried*	/iː/	*piece, believe*
	/e/	*friend*	/ɪə/	*pierce, fierce*
oa	/əʊ/	*coat, goal, approach*	/ɔː/	*abroad, board*
ou	/əʊ/	*soul, shoulder*	/uː/	*soup, routine*
	/aʊ/	*house, sprout*	/ɒ/	*cough*
	/ʌ/	*double, trouble, tough*	/ɔː/	*bought, nought*
ue	/uː/	*blue, due, sue*	/juː/	*sue, value, queue*
ui	/uː/	*fruit, suit, juice*	/ɪ/	*building, biscuit*
	/juː/	for some speakers: *suit*	/aɪ/	*guide*

Some combinations of vowel letters do not follow the 'naming' rule, as follows:

au	/ɔː/	*daughter, cause* (These tend towards /ɑː/ in G.A.)
	/ɑː/	*aunt, laugh, laughter* (These are pronounced /æ/ in G.A.)
	/ɒ/	*because, claustrophobia* (These tend towards /ɑː/ in G.A.)
eu	/uː/ or /juː/	*neutral, neuter*
	/jɔː/ or /jʊə/	for some speakers: *neuralgic, neurosis, Europe*
oi	/ɔɪ/	*coin, join, disappoint*
oo	/uː/	*food, boot*
	/ʌ/	*blood, flood*
	/ʊ/	*book, foot*

In addition, letter combinations composed of a vowel and a consonant (always *w* or *y*) are linked to particular sounds.

aw	/ɔː/	*jaw, flaw.* (These tend towards /ɑː/ in G.A.)
ay	/eɪ/	*today, way, say*
ew	/uː/ or /juː/	*new, knew, threw*
	/əʊ/	*sew*
ey	/iː/	*key*
	/eɪ/	*obey*
ow	/əʊ/	*own, thrown*
	/aʊ/	*town, crown*
oy	/ɔɪ/	*toy, boy, enjoy*

Table 8: Modifiers and preservatives

Certain letters modify or preserve other sounds within a word. The most important of these are outlined below.

The 'e effect'	At the end of a one-syllable word, a final *e* can make the preceding vowel 'say its name': *fat/fate, scent/scene, bit/bite, not/note, cut/cute*. (Exceptions to this rule, however, include some very common words, many ending in *-ve, -me* and *-ne*: *have, live, move, above, some, come, none, gone*.) A final *-le* can do the same: *tab/table, lad/ladle*
	The effect is sometimes preserved even if the *e* from the root form is no longer present and the end of the word has been changed: *complete/completion, smile/smiling*
The 'y effect'	This can be similar to the *e* effect: *lad/lady, tin/tiny*
'Double-consonant blockers'	When a consonant is doubled, the 'e effect' is usually lost: *fat/fatter, bit/bitten*. The 'y effect' is lost too: *mummy, daddy*, as is the 'le effect': *knob, noble, nobble*
'Extra-consonant blockers'	A similar effect is noticed if an extra different consonant is added: *produce/production, describe/description*
The 'r effect'	*r* can modify a preceding vowel sound: *cat/cart, pat/part*
The 'w effect'	*w* can change a preceding vowel (*hot/how, lot/low*) and a subsequent vowel (*work, war, world*)
The 'l effect'	*l* within a word can also change vowel quality (*bad/bald, cod/cold*), as can a double-*l* (compare the vowel sound in *pile* and *pill*). It can also 'sneak in', changing the vowel sound but keeping quiet: *half, calm*.

Appendix D

Further reading

The following books are recommended for further investigation into phonology, phonetics and pronunciation teaching:

Brazil, D. (1997) *The Communicative Value of Intonation in English*. Cambridge University Press.

Brazil, D. (1995) *A Grammar of Speech*. Oxford University Press.

Clark, J. and Yallop, C. (1995) *An Introduction to Phonetics and Phonology*. Blackwell.

Cruttenden, A. (Editor) (1994) *Gimson's Pronunciation of English*. Arnold.

Dalton, C. and Seidlhofer, B. (1994) *Pronunciation*. Oxford University Press.

Jones, D. (1960) *An Outline of English Phonetics*. Cambridge University Press.

Kenworthy, J. (1987) *Teaching English Pronunciation*. Longman.

Pennington, M. (1996) *Phonology in English Language Teaching*. Longman.

Roach, P. (1991) *English Phonetics and Phonology*. Cambridge University Press.

Swan, M. and Smith, B. (Editors) (1987) *Learner English*. Cambridge University Press.

Speak Out! (Newsletter of the IATEFL Pronunciation Special Interest Group)

Underhill, A. (1994) *Sound Foundations*. Heinemann.

Wells, J. C. (1990) *Longman Pronunciation Dictionary*. Longman.

The following books are recommended as sources of useful classroom teaching materials:

Baker, A. (1981) *Tree or Three?* (elementary) and *Ship or Sheep?* (intermediate). (Also *Introducing English Pronunciation*, which is a teacher's guide and notes for both books.) Cambridge University Press.

Baker, A. and Goldstein, S. (1990) *Pronunciation Pairs*. Cambridge University Press.

Bowler, B. and Cunningham, S. (1990) *Headway Intermediate Pronunciation*. (Also pre-intermediate and upper-intermediate levels, plus elementary level by Cunningham, S. and Moor, P. and *New Headway Pronunciation Course* (1999) by Cunningham, S. and Bowler, B.) Oxford University Press.

Bradford, B. (1988) *Intonation in Context* (upper intermediate to advanced). Cambridge University Press.

Brazil, D. (1994) *Pronunciation for Advanced Learners of English*. Cambridge University Press.

Bowen, T. and Marks, J. (1992) *The Pronunciation Book*. Longman.

Hancock, M. (1995) *Pronunciation Games*. Cambridge University Press.

Hewings, M. (1993) *Pronunciation Tasks* (pre-intermediate). Cambridge University Press.

Mortimer, C. (1985) *Elements of Pronunciation* (upper intermediate to proficiency). Cambridge University Press.

O'Connor, J. D. and Fletcher, C. (1989) *Sounds English* (intermediate to upper intermediate). Longman.

Ponsonby, M. (1982) *How Now Brown Cow* (intermediate to advanced). Prentice Hall.

Vaughan-Rees, M. (1994) *Rhymes and Rhythm* (intermediate). Prentice Hall.

Index